APPLYING SOCIAL WORK THEORY
A JOURNAL

APPLYING SOCIAL WORK THEORY
A JOURNAL

Barbara Bassot

BLOOMSBURY ACADEMIC
LONDON · NEW YORK · OXFORD · NEW DELHI · SYDNEY

BLOOMSBURY ACADEMIC

Bloomsbury Publishing Plc

50 Bedford Square, London, WC1B 3DP, UK
1385 Broadway, New York, NY 10018, USA
29 Earlsfort Terrace, Dublin 2, Ireland

BLOOMSBURY, BLOOMSBURY ACADEMIC and the Diana logo are trademarks of
Bloomsbury Publishing Plc

First published in Great Britain 2024

Copyright © Barbara Bassot 2024

Barbara Bassot has asserted her right to be identified as the author of this work
in accordance with the Copyright, Designs and Patents Act 1988.

All rights reserved. No part of this publication may be reproduced or transmitted in any forms or by any means, electronic or mechanical, including photocopying, recording, or any information storage or retrieval system, without prior permission in writing from the publishers.

Bloomsbury Publishing Plc does not have any control over, or responsibility for, any third-party websites referred to or in this book. All internet addresses given in this book were correct at the time of going to press. The author and publisher regret any inconvenience caused if addresses have changed or sites have ceased to exist, but can accept no responsibility for any such changes.

A catalogue record for this book is available from the British Library.

A catalog record for this book is available from the Library of Congress.

ISBN: PB: 978-1-3503-4410-5
       ePDF: 978-1-3503-4411-2
       eBook: 978-1-3503-4412-9

Typeset by Integra Software Services Pvt. Ltd.
Printed and bound in India.

To find out more about our authors and books visit www.bloomsbury.com and sign up for our newsletter.

Contents

	List of figures and tables	x
	Acknowledgements	xi
Introduction		1
	The structure of the book and how to use it	2
	What is theory and why bother with it?	5
	Challenges of applying theory to practice in social work	6
	Outline of contents	7

Part 1	**From theory to practice**	9
Chapter 1	**Psychodynamic approaches**	11
	A summary	11
Step 1	A short summary	15
Step 2	Applying psychodynamics to yourself	16
Step 3	A case study from social work practice to illustrate psychodynamics	18
Step 4	How some knowledge of psychodynamic theory can help you to understand more about Aeisha's case	19
Step 5	Applying psychodynamic theory to your experiences in the workplace	21
Chapter 2	**Attachment theory**	23
	A summary	23
Step 1	A short summary	27
Step 2	Applying attachment theory to yourself	28
Step 3	A case study from social work practice to illustrate attachment theory	30
Step 4	How some knowledge of attachment theory can help you to understand more about Charlie's case	31
Step 5	Applying attachment theory to your experiences in the workplace	33

Chapter 3	Cognitive-behavioural approaches	34
	A summary	34
Step 1	A short summary	38
Step 2	Applying cognitive-behavioural approaches to yourself	39
Step 3	A case study from social work practice to illustrate cognitive-behavioural approaches	41
Step 4	How some knowledge of cognitive-behavioural approaches can help you to understand more about Chloe's case	42
Step 5	Applying cognitive-behavioural approaches to your experiences in the workplace	45
Chapter 4	**Solution-focused approaches**	**46**
	A summary	46
Step 1	A short summary	49
Step 2	Applying solution-focused approaches to yourself	50
Step 3	A case study from social work practice to illustrate solution-focused approaches	53
Step 4	How some knowledge of solution-focused approaches can help you to understand more about Kadie's case	54
Step 5	Applying solution-focused approaches to your experiences in the workplace	56
Chapter 5	**Motivational interviewing (MI)**	**58**
	A summary	58
Step 1	A short summary	62
Step 2	Applying MI to yourself	63
Step 3	A case study from social work practice to illustrate MI	65
Step 4	How some knowledge of MI can help you to understand more about Peggy's case	66
Step 5	Applying MI to your experiences in the workplace	69
Chapter 6	**Strengths-based perspectives**	**72**
	A summary	72
Step 1	A short summary	76
Step 2	Applying strengths-based perspectives to yourself	77

Step 3	A case study from social work practice to illustrate strengths-based perspectives	79
Step 4	How some knowledge of strengths-based perspectives can help you to understand more about James' case	80
Step 5	Applying strengths-based perspectives to your experiences in the workplace	82

Chapter 7	**Systems theory**	**84**
	A summary	84
Step 1	A short summary	88
Step 2	Applying systems theory to yourself	89
Step 3	A case study from social work practice to illustrate systems theory	90
Step 4	How some knowledge of systems theory can help you to understand more about Kane's case	91
Step 5	Applying systems theory to your experiences in the workplace	93

Chapter 8	**Critical practice**	**95**
	A summary	95
Step 1	A short summary	99
Step 2	Applying critical practice to yourself	100
Step 3	A case study from social work practice to illustrate critical practice	101
Step 4	How some knowledge of critical practice can help you to understand more about social work in Oxtown	102
Step 5	Applying critical practice to your experiences in the workplace	105

Chapter 9	**Feminism**	**107**
	A summary	107
Step 1	A short summary	111
Step 2	Applying feminism to yourself	112
Step 3	A case study from social work practice to illustrate feminism	114
Step 4	How some knowledge of feminism can help you to understand more about Shazia and Nazir's situation	115
Step 5	Applying feminism to your experiences in the workplace	117

Chapter 10	Anti-oppressive practice	119
	A summary	119
Step 1	A short summary	123
Step 2	Applying anti-oppressive practice to yourself	124
Step 3	A case study from social work practice to illustrate anti-oppressive practice	126
Step 4	How some knowledge of anti-oppressive practice can help you to understand more about Geoffrey's case	127
Step 5	Applying anti-oppressive practice to your experiences in the workplace	129
Chapter 11	**Person-centred approaches**	**131**
	A summary	131
Step 1	A short summary	135
Step 2	Applying person-centred approaches to yourself	136
Step 3	A case study from social work practice to illustrate person-centred approaches	138
Step 4	How some knowledge of person-centred approaches can help you to understand more about Steven's case	139
Step 5	Applying person-centred approaches to your experiences in the workplace	141
Chapter 12	**Critically reflective practice**	**143**
	A summary	143
Step 1	A short summary	147
Step 2	Applying critically reflective practice to yourself	148
Step 3	A case study from social work practice to illustrate critically reflective practice	150
Step 4	How some knowledge of critically reflective practice can help you to understand more about Jude's case	151
Step 5	Applying critically reflective practice to your experiences in the workplace	153
Part 2	**From practice to theory**	**155**
	Jack	158
	Cleo	164
	The Garside-Rhodes family	171

Part 3	**From my own practice to theory**	177
	Further reading	198
	References	199
	Index	202

Figures and tables

Figures

Figure i.i	From theory to practice	2
Figure i.ii	From practice to theory	3
Figure i.iii	From my practice to theory	4
Figure 1.1	The three structural parts of the personality	12
Figure 2.1	Stages of attachment theory	24
Figure 3.1	Breaking vicious cycles through CBT	36
Figure 4.1	Elements of SFBT	48
Figure 5.1	A cycle of change	59
Figure 6.1	Six practice principles for a strengths-based approach	74
Figure 7.1	The three levels of systems theory	86
Figure 8.1	Critical practice	97
Figure 9.1	Aspects of feminism	109
Figure 10.1	Thompson's (2021) PCS analysis	121
Figure 11.1	Conditions for therapeutic change	132
Figure 12.1	The Integrated Reflective Cycle	144

Tables

Table 2.1	Jack – a summary of key words and phrases, and links with relevant theory	160
Table 2.2	Cleo – a summary of key words and phrases, and links with relevant theory	166
Table 2.3	The Garside-Rhodes family – a summary of key words and phrases, and links with relevant theory	173-174

Acknowledgements

I would like to thank Helen Caunce, my commissioning editor for asking me to write this book, which, as someone who has never been a social worker, was something I would not have contemplated. The link she made with two social work tutors from Leeds Beckett University (Emma Geddes and Rebecca O'Keefe) was vital in enabling me to write the book and my special thanks go to both of them for writing the case studies and for reviewing the manuscript for authenticity. I simply could not have written this book without you. I would also like to thank Becky Mutton and Emma Pritchard for their editorial support. My thanks also go to my family and friends for all their support along the way, especially to Martin Bassot for his excellent work on the diagrams and to Marc Bassot for his careful proofreading.

Introduction

You are probably reading this book because you are training to become a social worker and are a student on an undergraduate or postgraduate programme. You could also be someone undertaking an apprenticeship in social work. Whatever your method of training, a key part of your studies will be an examination of a range of different theoretical approaches that you will be expected to apply to professional social work practice. As your course progresses, you will build your practical knowledge during a range of placements where you will work with practitioners and the people they are supporting. Here, you will learn to apply your growing theoretical knowledge to social work practice.

To become an effective and knowledgeable social worker, you will need to be able to apply a wide range of theoretical approaches to the complex lives of those you will meet in professional practice. Debates continue regarding the terms used by professionals when referring to these people, and in this particular regard, we have opted to keep terminology very general. However, in certain settings, the term 'client' is used, and this is particularly appropriate when discussing theory that has its roots in counselling. Applying theory to practice in social work is no simple task, and you can often be faced with what seems like a large gap between the theories and approaches you are taught in university and the lived experiences of the service users you encounter in the workplace.

Applying theory to practice is often challenging and using a metaphor here is helpful. Imagine you are out walking and come across a wide, fast-flowing stream that you need to cross, but there is nothing there to help you get easily and safely to the other side. At this particular point, you may also regret wearing your brand-new trainers and best pair of jeans! You can't help but wish for some stepping stones to help you get to the other side. The overall purpose of this book is to provide the stepping stones you need to apply theory on one side of the stream to practice on the other. Taking these steps will not only benefit your future social work practice but will also enable you to show greater understanding in your assessed work at university.

The structure of the book and how to use it

This book is split into three parts, and in each part, a framework is used to help you to engage with a broad range of theories covered on many social work courses and apply them to practice.

Part 1 From theory to practice – five stepping stones (see Figure i.i)

Following an accessible summary of a particular theoretical approach

Step 1: Writing a short summary of the approach concerned and listing five key points

Step 2: Responding to reflective questions and exercises where you are asked to apply this approach to yourself

Step 3: A case study from social work practice to illustrate this approach

Step 4: A commentary on the case study using some key questions to help you to examine the case in relation to this approach

Step 5: Responding to a number of questions and exercises that help you apply this approach to your experiences in the workplace

There are twelve chapters in Part 1, each taking this five-step approach, where you will be asked to write a short summary of the approach and apply it to yourself first, through the use of reflective questions. An illustrative case study with a reflective discussion will help you take the important step of applying theory to work with individuals when you come into contact with them in the workplace. The theoretical summaries offered at the beginning of each chapter are what they say they are – summaries – and you will want to read them alongside other sources like Payne (2020, 2021), Teater (2020), Musson (2017), Beckett and Horner (2016) and Howe (2009). Each summary contains a brief critique of the theory in question. You shouldn't rely on this book alone as the source of your theoretical knowledge but see it as a starting point. The theories covered in Part 1 are designed to take you on a journey through social work

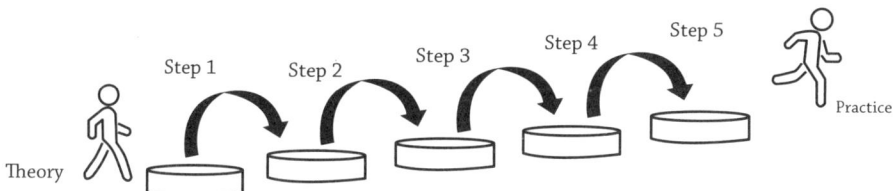

Figure i.i From theory to practice

theory, which is in part chronological. This starts with psychological approaches in Chapters 1 to 6, moving on to sociological approaches in Chapters 7 to 10 and finishing with approaches that can be said to bring the two together in Chapters 11 and 12.

Part 2 From practice to theory – three stepping stones (see Figure i.ii)

Step 1: A complex case study from social work practice

Step 2: Selecting which theories might apply by identifying key words and phrases and posing some questions, followed by a table showing the links made

Step 3: A discussion of how particular theories apply

Part 2 contains three complex and contrasting case studies and the three stepping stones above are used to help you examine how theory can help you understand more about the lives of those you are supporting. The case studies show that no single theory can offer every insight into an individual's life, and that often knowledge of multiple theories will be needed in order to offer the best support.

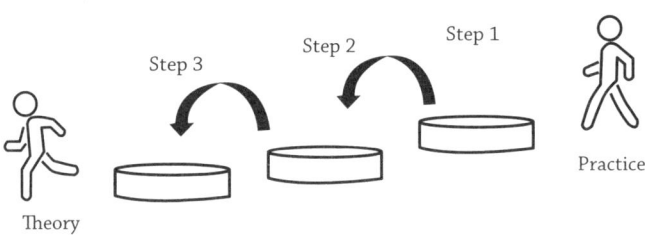

Figure i.ii From practice to theory

Part 3 From my own practice to theory – three stepping stones (see Figure i.iii)

This is your opportunity to follow the three stepping stones from Part 2 in order to devise your own case studies from your experience in the workplace.

Step 1: Write your own complex case study from your experience, using the headings provided

Step 2: Key questions to help you examine which theories apply to the case with space to write notes

Step 3: Space to write a discussion of how theories apply to your own case

At the end of Part 3, there is a full list of references and a reading list to point you to further sources of relevant literature.

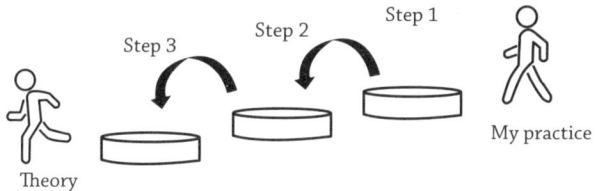

Figure i.iii From my practice to theory

The book has a journal format and is designed as a book you write in. This is done for three main reasons.

1. Writing helps to develop our understanding. Early in my academic career, I attended a writers' seminar where the leader of the session (a widely published professor) said that he writes in order to understand. Up to that point, I had always assumed that people wrote about things because they had a lot of knowledge, and they already understood a lot. At the time, this was something of a revelation to me and, following this, I found that the more I wrote, the more I understood.
2. Research in neuroscience shows that writing by hand stimulates a particular part at the base of the brain called the reticular activating system, or the RAS (Pérez Alonso, 2015). The RAS acts as a filter for information that the brain needs to process and ensures that we pay more attention to what we are actively focusing on at a given moment. So writing sharpens our focus and is an important tool in any challenging academic work such as applying theory to practice. It means we are much more likely to remember something if we write about it, and it is more likely to stick in our minds as it cements our understanding.
3. Writing in a journal helps us to take a questioning approach. At various points in the book, you will see some key questions with space for you to write your responses. Working with people in any professional context is rarely simple and straightforward, and social work is certainly no exception to this. It is all too easy to make assumptions and jump to conclusions, and this is something that professional practitioners need to guard against. They can do this better when they take a slower, questioning approach using critical reflection.

In general, the process of writing by hand forces us to slow down because most of us can type more quickly than we can write. This means we take time to reflect, which allows our knowledge and understandings to grow. So please write in this book! In addition, the book takes a questioning approach throughout, and this is an important aid to your academic development. Theories should not be accepted at face value and need to be critiqued. Posing the kinds of questions offered will help you to write more analytically, which should help you to gain higher marks in your assessed work.

What is theory and why bother with it?

At this point, it is good to clarify what we mean by the term 'theory'. 'Theory' might be a word that we think we understand, but in fact many of us would find it difficult to give a clear definition of it if we were asked. Surprising as this might sound, a definition of theory is something that academics and tutors do not always agree on and continue to debate. Thomas (2017) discusses five different meanings of the word 'theory' as follows:

1. A generalizing or explanatory model – this is theory that draws together findings or observations in order to put forward general propositions of how things are perceived;
2. The 'thinking side' of practice – often used in the applied social sciences (including social work) and referred to as 'reflective practice' or 'practical theory' where explanations emerge from and are grounded in professional practice;
3. A developing body of explanation – theory from this perspective keeps knowledge in a particular area moving forward;
4. Scientific theory – explains ideas as a series of statements that can be tested, so that predictions can be made. In the social sciences (including social work), this is becoming less common;
5. Grand theory – something that seeks to explain the nature of mankind and society broadly. Examples include Marxism and Freudian theory. (Drawn from Thomas, 2017: 98.)

Most of these five types of theory will be considered in this book, with the exception of scientific theory.

When asking my own students what theory is, many have responded initially by saying, 'It's someone's idea'. But theory is much more than that. My own view is that theory is an individual's (or two people's or even a group of people's) explanation of a particular phenomenon. It has a sound basis in research, rather like Thomas' first point. In addition, it will have been published in academic sources, such as well-respected journals. Theory by its very nature is often abstract, and my favourite quote in relation to the essence of theory comes from the seminal writer and theorist, Kurt Lewin. Lewin (1951: 169) states, 'There's nothing so practical as good theory', which serves to make the whole idea of theory accessible and useful. As one of the founders of social and organizational psychology, Lewin was interested in theory that could be applied in practice, which led him to develop the strategy of action research with its focus on bringing about change in organizations. This is theory that seeks explanations from practice (rather like Thomas' second point), which in turn continues to develop a body of knowledge as things change (Thomas' third point).

Lewin argues that good theory is practical, which means it can be applied easily. In discussions with my own students about the value of particular theories, some have said things like 'But this just seems like common sense' or even 'This is obvious' and are tempted to dismiss the theory in question in order to find something more complex. For me, this is a hallmark of good theory! Some of the theory covered in this book may be easier to apply than others, but don't be deceived into thinking that if you find a particular theory easy to apply, it isn't worthwhile; it probably is.

Social work is a very practical profession, and it can be tempting at times to wonder why so much emphasis is placed on theory, and maybe even why you need to bother with theory at all. Some of you might be thinking that getting experience is the most important thing and that this is what will make you an effective practitioner. But this is only one angle on professional practice, and another is the understanding of people and how and why they behave in the ways they do. I often say to my own students that there are usually reasons why people are as they are, and theory really helps us to understand people better.

Challenges of applying theory to practice in social work

Applying theory to practice in social work can be challenging for a number of reasons. There is no doubt that people are complex and can face multiple challenges in life. There is no single theoretical approach that can universally explain how and why people experience things in particular ways and respond in the way they do. People are all different and how they deal with similar situations can vary a great deal. A strategy that helps one person or family can hinder another, even though their circumstances might on the surface appear to be the same. It is good to beware of anyone who says something like 'I use this approach all the time with everyone, and it always works.' It may well only be a matter of time before they are proved wrong, or worse, they realize that their practice has completely stagnated.

In addition, no single theory can offer all the explanations needed for one case. In many instances, practitioners need to be able to draw on particular aspects of a range of different theories to reach the multiple explanations they need to inform their practice. This means that the best support can be offered to those they are working with. It also means work is never boring!

Outline of contents

Part 1 From theory to practice – five stepping stones

This covers twelve of the most common theoretical approaches studied on social work courses. They are

1 Psychodynamic approaches
2 Attachment theory
3 Cognitive-behavioural approaches
4 Solution-focused approaches
5 Motivational interviewing
6 Strengths-based perspectives
7 Systems theory
8 Critical practice
9 Feminism
10 Anti-oppressive practice
11 Person-centred approaches
12 Critically reflective practice

Part 2 From practice to theory – three stepping stones

Here, three complex case studies are examined in relation to a range of theories.

Part 3 From my own practice to theory – three stepping stones

This offers you space to write your own case studies from your time in the workplace and to examine them in relation to theory.

Finally, this is not necessarily a book to work through from start to finish. It might work better for you to use certain sections in particular modules, and to use Part 3 while you are spending time in the workplace. Please be flexible and use this book as and when it suits you best.

Good luck with your studies!
Barbara Bassot

Part 1
From theory to practice

CHAPTER 1

Psychodynamic approaches

A summary

Our journey through social work theory starts with psychodynamic approaches, which became influential from the 1920s onwards. These were initially inspired by the work of Sigmund Freud who is seen as the founder of psychoanalysis. Freud argued that the unconscious along with early life experiences had strong links with subsequent human behaviour and that many of the causes of this behaviour were to be found in the mind. The mind is full of mental energy which renders it dynamic, hence the term 'psychodynamics'. Our constantly changing and dynamic minds have an impact on how we think, feel and behave at any point in the situations we experience in life. Freud asserted that through a process of analysis in therapy, clients could be helped to understand the impact of the mind on their behaviour. This meant in turn that people could address their issues and difficulties more effectively, which represented the birth of what we now call 'talking therapies'. The focus of psychodynamic approaches is firmly on the individual and at the time this emerged was seen as a distinct move away from an emphasis on the economic and social problems of the day.

Some of the terms used in psychodynamics have made their way into everyday speech, whilst others are most often only used by professional practitioners. A selection of key terms is outlined here.

Id, ego and superego

These are the three structural parts of the personality as shown in Figure 1.1. The id is concerned with our basic needs as human beings; our need to stay alive, to experience pleasure and to avoid pain. These needs are essential for our survival, they operate powerfully at an unconscious level and demand to be met immediately. However, in reality, this cannot always happen and here the ego begins to be in evidence, which steps in to regulate the ways in which these needs can be met through our relationships with others. As children develop, so does their superego, as parents and significant others tell them what they can and cannot do. The superego helps children to develop a conscience as they internalize what is good, bad, right and wrong.

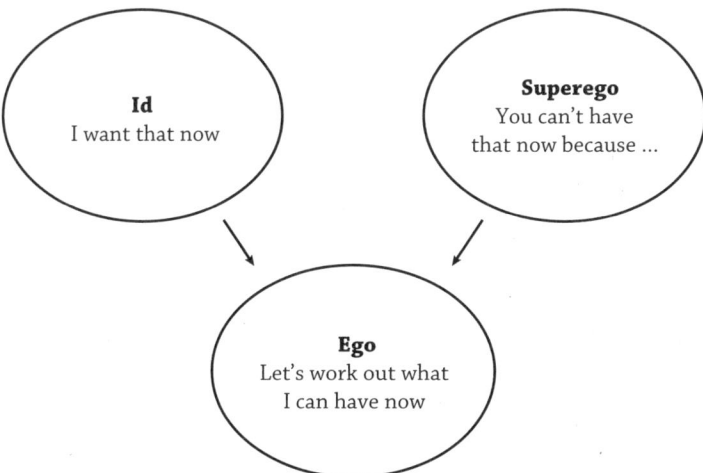

Figure 1.1 The three structural parts of the personality

Through effective parenting, children learn to manage the id by the development of a strong ego and superego, and as a result, they are likely to go on and live happy and satisfying lives. However, those who do not experience support in this process will often struggle. For example, those who cannot control the id because of the lack of development of the ego can face difficulties as they try to satisfy their insatiable basic needs. Without a strong superego, they may act at times as if they lack a 'moral compass'.

Defence mechanisms

We all use defence mechanisms to help us cope with difficult emotions and experiences that we find painful to think about. These are natural coping mechanisms that we use in a wide variety of ways. For example, the pain of a close family bereavement might be so intense that we immerse ourselves in work or leisure. Equally, a serious injury to ourselves or to someone we know and love, might be so painful to recall that we try to blot it out through activity. This is called repression.

Displacement is also a strong defence mechanism, and this is where feelings experienced in one situation are displaced onto another. For example, as a teenager, I might have had a terrible day at school and then be angry and irritable at home with my close family who have had nothing to do with my actual experience.

Denial is when we are unable to admit to ourselves how we feel, and in difficult situations, we 'put on a brave face' and pretend that nothing is wrong or even that we don't care, when in fact we care deeply. For example, if we apply for a job we really want and then don't get it, we might use denial in order to cope with feelings of rejection, perhaps even convincing ourselves that we didn't really want the job anyway.

Projection is another defence mechanism where we attack or even make fun of people who are doing things that deep down we know we would like to do ourselves. For example, we might tease or even ridicule our co-workers for undertaking a course, when actually we would really like to do the course ourselves if we could.

Free association

Through his clinical work, Freud discovered that giving people opportunities to speak freely about their difficulties often meant that they were better able to cope with their situations and experiences. This free speaking, or free association as it is termed, means that thoughts and feelings that have been repressed or denied can come to the surface and be dealt with by the client. Although this all happens within the parameters of the non-judgemental therapeutic relationship, it can cause anxiety, which in turn can lead to resistance on the part of the client.

Transference and counter-transference

In our relationships with others, we often have thoughts and feelings that are based on experiences we have had in the past, which is something that we are not necessarily conscious of. For example, a trainee social worker who is required to gain workplace experience in situations that they have found difficult in the past (for example, in a hospital or social care setting) might find them upsetting or even irritating because of all the thoughts and feelings from their past that are brought to the surface. This is transference. Counter-transference is when the practitioner finds themselves thinking about a client in a certain way based on previous repressed feelings from experiences in their personal life. For example, they might feel positively or negatively towards the person they are working with because they remind them of someone from their past, such as a beloved family member, a difficult teacher or a bully at school.

Like all theories, psychodynamics has been critiqued for a number of reasons. In general terms, theories that focus on the individual (Chapters 1 to 6) face criticism for a lack of focus on the social context. Those that focus on the social context (Chapters 7 to 10) face criticism because they fail to account for individual differences. Even the most well-known and respected theory has its critics, and it is important to accept nothing at face value. Other criticisms of psychodynamic theory are that it is strongly deterministic and views behaviour as something that is caused by unconscious factors that we have no control over. This is particularly difficult for people working in the helping professions who seek to support people to try to have more control over their lives through personal agency. Gabbard (2014) acknowledges the notion of determinism but also argues that this does not apply to all behaviours or symptoms.

Psychodynamic theory has also faced criticism for failing to address the cultural context (Robbins et al., 2006) and is also accused of being sexist (Berzoff, 2011). It seems clear that Freud believed that women were inferior to men, and that men had stronger superegos than women, making women more prone to anxiety. The work has also been criticized for a lack of reference to issues of racism (Mattei, 2011) and homophobia, but bearing in mind when Freud was writing, this is not surprising.

As a social worker, you are not a therapist, but it seems clear that psychodynamics can help you to understand some of the underlying causes of a client's behaviour. Understanding more about why people might behave as they do will help on two levels. First, it will help you to discern the kind of support the client might need and the issues they might need to face up to and begin to address. Second, on a personal level, it will mean you are much less likely to take things too personally, for example, when a client rejects your help or acts in an aggressive way. This is important for your own stress levels, self-esteem and longevity in the profession. Many people would say that there are usually reasons why people behave as they do, and psychodynamics would certainly bear this out.

 **Step 1** A short summary

Now write a short summary of psychodynamic theory by listing five key points:

1

2

3

4

5

Now summarize why you feel it might be important for you as a social worker to have an understanding of psychodynamics.

 **Step 2** Applying psychodynamics to yourself

Which aspects of the three structural aspects of personality can you recognize in yourself? Make some notes under each of these headings.

Id

Ego

Superego

What kind of defence mechanisms can you recognize in yourself, and how have you used them to help you to cope with difficult life experiences? Try and give an example of each of the following:

Repression

Displacement

Denial

Projection

What were the positive effects of using these?

Were there negative effects too and if so, what were they?

Now think about the experiences of people you know well. Do any of them display any of these defence mechanisms, and if so, how?

Can you identify situations where you have experienced transference and counter-transference? Make some notes under these headings.

Transference

Counter-transference

 **Step 3**   # A case study from social work practice to illustrate psychodynamics

Aeisha (23) is expecting her second child and you are working with her to complete a pre-birth parenting assessment. This is proving to be a difficult piece of work, as Aeisha seems reluctant to speak with you.

Aeisha is the eldest of three children and has a complex history. She and her siblings were taken into care when Aeisha was 11 and her younger brothers were 3 and 5. Initially, the children lived together in a foster placement, but Aeisha's behaviour became difficult to manage and the foster carers decided that they could no longer care for her. Aeisha's brothers remained in their placement and the carers later became their Special Guardians. Aeisha has not had any contact with her brothers for many years. After leaving her first foster placement, Aeisha moved between foster care and residential homes, where she experienced sexual exploitation and substance misuse issues.

Aeisha's first child, Destiny, was born when Aeisha was 18. It was not known at the time who Destiny's father was. Due to the high level of concern about Aeisha's 'chaotic' lifestyle, the court ordered that Aeisha and Destiny would live in a mother and baby foster placement after Destiny was born. Aeisha was very competent in caring for Destiny but struggled with living in the foster placement. After a positive drugs test, Aeisha left the placement and Destiny remained in foster care. Aeisha continued to attend contact with Destiny three times per week until the court decided that it was in Destiny's best interests to be adopted without Aeisha's consent. Aeisha now receives an annual letter from Destiny's adopters but has not seen her since her adoption. Aeisha did not receive any post-adoption support after Destiny was adopted.

Aeisha is in a new relationship with a partner who works as a chef at a local restaurant, where she is employed as bar staff. Aeisha has stopped using substances and does not accept that you need to have any information about her pregnancy or the new baby. Whenever you mention Destiny, Aeisha becomes extremely agitated and changes the subject.

Step 4 — How some knowledge of psychodynamic theory can help you to understand more about Aeisha's case.

What evidence might there be of Aeisha's id, ego and superego?

At many points in her life, Aeisha's id has instinctively tried to help her to avoid immense pain. Her chaotic life and multiple carers are unlikely to have given her the ongoing support she needed to develop her ego that would help her to manage her id. In particular, her drug misuse could be evidence of a weak superego.

How might Aeisha's early life experiences be having an impact on her behaviour?

It seems clear that Aeisha had a very difficult early life, going into care when she was 11 with her two younger brothers. Even though life at home must have been very difficult for her, being removed from there is likely to have been traumatic, as much of what she knew was taken away. She may have been caring for her younger brothers since they were born, something that can be very difficult to relinquish to strangers. Because of her behaviour (she was entering teenagehood at the time), she was unable to stay with her brothers so was removed again, no doubt causing further trauma. By contrast, her brothers gained special guardianship, giving them greater security and protection, something that Aeisha herself may have longed for. Over time, she lost all her close family through no fault of her own, both her parent (or parents) and her brothers, so she probably has a huge sense of loss. The subsequent sexual exploitation probably made her question whom she could trust, and some substance misuse issues followed.

How might her more recent life experiences affect her?

It is likely that Aeisha continued to experience feelings of rejection following Destiny's birth. She did not disclose who Destiny's father was and we are left wondering if Destiny was a result of Aeisha having been sexually exploited while in care. It seems on the surface that Aeisha was trying to be a good mother and she was described as being very competent with Destiny, but her many struggles with living in care continued, until her drug use was evident again and she left Destiny in foster care. It is hard to imagine the range of emotions that Aeisha might have been feeling when, without her consent, the court decided that Destiny should be adopted. They could include heartbreak, despondency, hopelessness and despair. In addition, she may also have felt a heavy burden of guilt in leaving Destiny, knowing the impact that similar experiences had had on her own life. In spite of her efforts in trying to care for Destiny and visiting her regularly, she may also have felt powerless in being able to have any influence over her own future and Destiny's. Because there was no support offered to Aeisha to help her cope with the trauma of Destiny's adoption, she is unlikely to have processed how she feels through free association.

What words could be used to describe Aeisha's emotions and why?

Aeisha is likely to be experiencing a wide range of emotions as a result of her early and ongoing life experiences. She has experienced a lot of rejection in her life, perhaps even to the point of feeling abandoned. Over time, she has been separated from all the people she was close to and may well have had times when she felt completely alone. Feelings of rejection may well have made her feel inferior, unworthy and lacking in self-esteem. In addition, sexual exploitation could make her feel angry, violated and victimized.

How does Aeisha seem to act out these childhood experiences in the present?

Aeisha seems to be using different defence mechanisms to help her cope with her current situation. She cannot bear to talk about Destiny, which probably shows that her feelings have been repressed, as they were too painful to face at the time, and she received no support in doing so. This was added to the pain of being separated from her brothers and her own parent or parents when she was younger. Aeisha has probably got used to blotting out how she feels in order to cope with the multiple rejections she has experienced in her life and may also have misused drugs to do this. In addition, she probably lives with feelings of guilt in relation to leaving Destiny.

Aeisha also seems to be in denial regarding aspects of her life experiences. She cannot see why you need to be involved in discussing her pregnancy. She now has a new life, job and partner and refuses to see how her past is relevant. Undoubtedly, Aeisha is reminded of her past experiences with social workers when she meets with you. The feelings she had when meeting social workers in the past come back to the surface through the process of transference, and she is reminded of some of the most difficult times in her life. Again, she tries to repress her feelings and deny what is happening, as she changes the subject.

Step 5 — Applying psychodynamic theory to your experiences in the workplace

Think about an experience you have had in the workplace where psychodynamic theory could provide some helpful explanations. Here are some questions you could ask, with space for your responses below.

What evidence is there of the individual's id, ego and superego?

Describe the defence mechanisms they are displaying (e.g. repression, displacement, denial, projection).

Is there any evidence of transference on the part of the individual and, if so, how did you recognize this?

Have you experienced any counter-transference working with this individual? If so, describe it here.

What kind of support might they need from you in the light of all of this and how might you best work with them?

CHAPTER 2

Attachment theory

A summary

Attachment theory was first developed by John Bowlby in the late 1960s and emerged from his work and practice in the UK as a child psychiatrist. Bowlby's initial work was heavily influenced by psychoanalysis, but by the time his work on attachment theory was first published (Bowlby, 1969), he was also interested in a wide range of developmental sciences, including cognitive psychology and systems theory. Mary Ainsworth and her colleagues later expanded on Bowlby's work in the 1970s (Ainsworth et al., 1978), revealing more about the profound impact of attachment on behaviour. At the present time, attachment theory is still seen as offering important explanations of aspects of early child development and giving valuable insights into the behaviour of adults, particularly in relation to emotional and mental wellbeing. This means that it can be described as seminal – a theory that has stood the test of time, continues to be relevant and has strongly influenced later theoretical developments. More recently, attachment theory is also being influenced by progress in neuroscience and the human brain's capacity, and indeed its need, to develop from stimulation by experience (Blakemore and Frith, 2005).

Babies are born with a range of behaviours that help them to survive in a world where they have no control over what happens to them and are totally dependent on others. They can sense when they are hungry, tired, cold, hot, in pain, frightened or distressed and their behavioural response to all of these is to cry. At any specific time, parents and carers are left with the job of trying to discern which of these symptoms is the cause – not an easy task! Babies cry in order to attract the attention of the caregiver, who then comes to their aid. Crying then is an attachment behaviour that is designed to link the infant with their carer. Bowlby argued that if the caregiver is sensitive and reasonably reliable, the baby will develop a secure attachment with them.

As a baby grows, attachments change (as shown in Figure 2.1). In the first two months of life, a baby shows no attachment to a particular caregiver and is said to be in the pre-attachment phase. For example, when a new-born baby has tummy ache, they won't mind who picks them up to 'wind' them. The important thing is that the pain goes away. But from 3 to 7 months, they begin to show a preference for primary and secondary caregivers – the indiscriminate phase. From 7 months, they start to exhibit a secure attachment to one specific caregiver (the discriminate phase), and from 10 months to 3 years, they begin to develop bonds with others during the multiple phase. Building secure attachments is especially important in the formative years, notably up to the age of around 5.

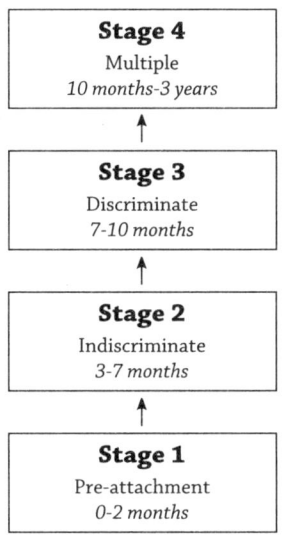

Figure 2.1 Stages of attachment theory

Attachment signifies an important and growing emotional bond between the baby and caregivers and Bowlby argued that this has an enormous impact on the child's life. Even in the early days of providing for a baby's basic physical needs (e.g. feeding, changing their nappies), other aspects of care are important, such as cuddling, talking, singing and having eye contact, and all of these help emotional attachments to grow and mean that a baby feels safe, secure and loved. These seemingly small actions mean that the caregiver's mind engages with the baby's developing mind in what psychologists call intersubjectivity as they share their experiences. For example, a caregiver smiles and a baby smiles back; on a basic level, they connect with each other as human beings, but at a deeper level, there is a meeting of their minds. No attachment is perfect because human beings are involved, and Winnicott (1960) famously spoke of mothers needing only to be 'good enough' for their children to thrive. Children who have secure attachments are more likely to grow up to be happy and confident with high levels of self-esteem. They feel loved and have a sense of their own value and self-worth.

Sadly, many children do not form secure attachments with their caregivers for a wide variety of reasons, and as a social worker, you will often see evidence of this in your professional practice. This is because parental care is sometimes inconsistent, unpredictable and, in extreme cases, neglectful and even abusive. This means some babies and children grow up experiencing high levels of anxiety, because they don't know what to expect. As children grow, they learn to adapt their behaviour to get a positive response, whether this is to keep quiet to avoid someone's anger (known as an avoidant attachment style) or to 'play up' to try to get their attention (known as an ambivalent attachment style, because often their needs remain unmet because of the lack of interest of the caregiver). If a baby or child has parents who are unpredictable in their responses, for example, because of alcohol or drug abuse, or mental health issues, they simply don't know what to expect and do not know how to adapt their behaviour accordingly. They develop disorganized attachment and become uncertain, fearful and insecure.

Attachment theory, like all other theories, has its critics, particularly in relation to three areas. First, any theory that argues that things happen in a particular sequence or within an identified time frame will always face questions regarding whether or not this is always the case and the same can be said of attachment theory. Critics of attachment theory argue that it seems to restrict or even fix child development within certain age boundaries, which has led to an acceptance of it as being evident throughout life (Sudbery and Whitaker, 2019).

Second, attachment theory can be said to place too much emphasis on the role of the primary caregiver, particularly the mother. Following the Second World War, Bowlby's assertion of the love of a mother as a biological need influenced discussions about, and subsequent policy decisions related to, the desirability of mothers working outside the home (Vicedo, 2011). This was particularly the case in the US but also in the UK. This claim placed a strong emotional demand on mothers, especially bearing in mind that during the war many children in the UK were evacuated and thereby removed from their close family members, in particular their mothers. Men returning from the war were encouraged to return to the labour market to support their families, which also put pressure on women to stay at home with their children. Of course, widows (and obviously there were many of them) often did not have this choice. More recently, attachment theory has been criticized by feminists as 'attributing blame and causality to mothers' (Wendt, 2016: 19), with some seeing it as an attack on working mothers.

Third, the universality of attachment theory is questioned (Hazan and Shaver, 1994). In many respects, it can be described as a Western middle-class approach and, of course, many people do not fit into this demographic. Attachment theory does not consider issues of ethnicity or social context and the effects that such things as marginalization and poverty can have on family life.

Whether a child has secure attachments or otherwise, over time, their experiences become internalized and form part of their psychological make-up. In a sense, they only know what they have experienced and their relationships with others inform and even shape how they interact with others. It is very common to meet adults who mirror the experiences of their own upbringing when they have their own children. In many ways, being a parent is the hardest job in the world, with very little training and one that people are catapulted into on a particular day and at a specific moment in time, usually with no going back. If the parent has the good fortune to have had caring and loving primary carers that they have (or had) a secure attachment to, they will have experienced more of how to form a secure attachment with their own child than someone who hasn't been as fortunate as them.

However, thankfully this does not automatically mean that an individual's life is completely predictable, and we can probably all think of people who had certain experiences as a child who later rejected the option of living their life in a similar way. For example, the child of an alcoholic parent, who decides never to drink any alcohol at all because of seeing and living with its negative effects, or the son or daughter whose parent is in prison, who decides not to offend because of the distressing separation it has caused. This is certainly something to be grateful for, especially in a profession like social work, because if not, what hope would there be for people, and how would we be able to continue with the work? Thankfully, many people have a capacity for change and can thrive with the care and support of others, even when their early years might not have been as positive as they might have been.

 **A short summary**

Now write a short summary of attachment theory by listing five key points:

1

2

3

4

5

Now summarize why you feel it might be important for you as a social worker to have an understanding of attachment theory.

Step 2 — Applying attachment theory to yourself

Think about some of the important relationships you had as you were growing up. Which do you feel were the most significant and why?

Which relationships were positive?

Were any of them negative and if so, why?

Can you recognize any aspects of different types of attachment in your own experiences? Here are some examples:
- Secure – balanced, well-rounded, confident, in tune with emotions of self and others
- Avoidant – ill at ease with emotions, prefer to be practical and get on with things, playing down own needs, prefer to be at a distance rather than close to people, often reserved
- Ambivalent – wanting the attention of others, under-confident, demanding
- Disorganized – aggressive, controlling, fearful, anxious

How have these affected your relationships with others as an adult?

Now think about the experiences of people you know well. Do any of them display any of these attachment behaviours and if so, how?

Step 3 — A case study from social work practice to illustrate attachment theory

Charlie (17) is the mother of Harry (3 weeks). Charlie lives with her parents, Anthony and Jill. Charlie did not realize she was pregnant until she was 19 weeks' gestation, and this came as a big surprise to her. She has not told anyone who Harry's father is. Charlie wanted to complete her college course and progress to university away from home. She felt low and tearful during her pregnancy.

Charlie considered a termination but was persuaded by Jill to continue with the pregnancy. Charlie had a difficult birth with Harry, which resulted in an emergency caesarean section. Charlie has needed a lot of help from Jill and Anthony in caring for Harry due to this procedure. Charlie's college made a referral for extra support for her very late in pregnancy, recognizing she did not want to talk about her baby and seeing her mood worsen.

You visit Charlie and Harry for the first time and notice that Charlie appears withdrawn. She doesn't look at you or speak. Jill is the person who is holding Harry when you arrive and she answers all your initial questions, even though you direct these to Charlie. You ask how Harry got his name and Charlie shrugs. Jill says, 'We decided as a family. Harry was Charlie's grandad's name.'

Harry begins to cry a few minutes into the visit and Charlie does not appear to notice. Jill says immediately, 'He'll be getting a little bit hungry, it's eleven o'clock', and she passes Harry to Charlie to go and make a bottle of formula milk. Charlie does hold Harry and tries to comfort him by rocking him. You notice she doesn't look directly at Harry and says 'Shhhh, shhhh' loudly and appears nervous and unsure.

Jill reappears and takes Harry immediately. Jill looks directly at Harry, giving good eye contact, and talks to him softly whilst beginning to feed him. You observe that Charlie does not look at Harry for the remainder of the visit but becomes a little brighter when you ask about college. Charlie says she wants to go back soon to continue her studies.

Step 4 — How some knowledge of attachment theory can help you to understand more about Charlie's case

What signs are there that Charlie might not be starting to build a strong attachment with Harry?

Charlie does not seem to be paying any attention to Harry, even when he starts to cry. She only holds Harry when her Mum, Jill, goes to prepare a bottle of formula milk. She tries to comfort Harry, but there is no eye contact between them. She doesn't cuddle or rock him to try and comfort him but instead just wants him to be quiet.

Which aspects of Charlie's pregnancy and Harry's delivery could indicate some potential difficulties in her current relationship with Harry?

Charlie only found out she was pregnant after 19 weeks and was clearly not expecting this. She has not told anyone who the father is and, while we don't know the reasons for this, we can assume that Charlie feels he has no part to play in their lives, at least at the moment. Equally, we don't know the circumstances of Harry's conception, but we do know that it was completely unplanned. She thought about a termination, but Jill persuaded her not to do this. We have to ask ourselves whether Charlie really wanted to have a baby at all, especially at this particular point in her life, when she had some clear plans for her future.

Following a difficult time in labour, Harry was delivered by an emergency caesarean section. This constitutes major invasive surgery, which can take, on average, six weeks to recover from. At this point, it is very likely that Charlie is still experiencing some physical pain as well as being unable to move around easily and to lift anything heavier than Harry.

In what ways might Charlie resent Harry, which could result in attachment difficulties?

Charlie had some clear plans for her future, which involved moving away to go to university. This would have been an important way of helping her to gain more independence and she might resent Harry for stopping her from doing this. She might also resent the physical pain Harry has caused her to experience, both while in labour and as a result of the caesarean section. She might be starting to feel the enormity of the responsibility that she now has for Harry's life and the dramatic and long-lasting change that Harry has brought to her life.

What might be stopping Charlie from developing a strong attachment with Harry?

Undoubtedly Jill is well-meaning, but it also seems fair to say that she could in effect be stopping Charlie from developing a strong attachment with Harry, simply because she seems to be doing everything that needs to be done for Harry without involving Charlie where she can. You could even say that Jill is taking over and that perhaps she wanted the baby more than Charlie herself did because she dissuaded her from having a termination.

Is it too late for Charlie to bond with Harry?

Definitely not. At the moment, Harry really doesn't mind who comforts him, feeds him, changes his nappy, and so on. But as time goes on, this will begin to matter much more, and Charlie needs to be given the opportunity to build a strong attachment with Harry. She will also need support in doing this, which will probably involve some careful negotiation with Jill.

How might things develop if Charlie can't develop a strong attachment with Harry?

If things continue as they are, Harry will enter the discriminate phase and begin to show that he prefers to be cared for by Jill, and this could lead to Charlie feeling rejected. A lack of attachment with Charlie could also lead to Harry feeling anxious, insecure and even unwanted in the future. This could present itself in a lack of confidence or challenging behaviour as Harry grows up.

 **Step 5**   Applying attachment theory to your experiences in the workplace

Think about an experience you have had in the workplace where attachment theory could provide some helpful explanations. Here are some questions you could ask, with space for your responses below.

What kind of attachment behaviour is the individual showing (secure, avoidant, ambivalent, disorganized)?

What is the evidence for this?

What kind of support might they need from you in the light of this and how might you best work with them?

Attachment theory   33

CHAPTER 3

Cognitive-behavioural approaches

A summary

As the term suggests, cognitive-behavioural approaches (often referred to as cognitive-behavioural therapy or CBT) suggest a merging of insights from cognitive and behavioural psychology. The emphasis here remains firmly on the individual and the ways in which the mind influences human behaviour, in complex and often automatic ways. In order to understand more about it, we first need to examine some of the history behind each of the approaches.

Behavioural approaches began to be explored in the 1920s through the work of Watson and Raynor (1920). Their experiments studied the links between stimulus and response and were carried out on babies. For example, babies were deliberately startled to see how they responded over time, sometimes causing previously placid babies to cry from fear and distress. These experiments would be seen as completely inappropriate today and even cruel. Other famous experiments were those of Pavlov (1928) and his dogs, which initially salivated when they smelt food (classical conditioning) and were then trained to salivate simply when a bell was rung (operant conditioning). These would also be seen as inappropriate today by many, especially by dog lovers and animal rights activists. These kinds of experiments showed that behaviour can be learned, and by the 1970s, some of these ideas had been developed into social learning theory by Bandura (1977) who also argued that people process information through mediation and observation. This means that they can model their behaviour on others, for better or for worse.

The premise of behavioural psychology is that behaviours are learned, and it is important to assess what is causing current behaviour and the reasons behind it. To carry out this assessment, behaviourists often use the ABC model.

A – antecedent, what happens before the behaviour?
B – behaviour, the behaviour itself (described in some detail)
C – consequences, what happens immediately after the behaviour?

The emphasis is on the present and not on the past, and in particular on how behaviour can be modified, which can be done by changing what happens either before or after the behaviour under scrutiny. The most effective and widely recognized behaviour modification technique is praise.

Behaviourists are not interested in the link between the stimulus and response but cognitive psychologists are. Like Bandura, they appreciate the ability of the mind to act as a mediator in order to process information. They understand that experiences are interpreted by different people in different ways and acknowledge that the mind can distort things that are real and imaginary. Such thinking is not new as the writing of Shakespeare shows. In Act II, sc. ii, Hamlet says, 'There is nothing either good or bad, but thinking makes it so', as he reflects on his physical imprisonment by Denmark and the King, but also on the mental imprisonment of his mind.

Cognitive psychologists understand that the way we think affects the way we feel. We have all met people who we might describe as 'glass half empty'. They tend to view situations from a negative position, thinking about the worst that can happen and what could go wrong. They are often cynical, can be pessimistic and might struggle with life's challenges, perhaps facing issues such as anxiety and depression. By contrast, there are 'glass half full' people who take the opposite approach. They tend to see life from a positive standpoint, see the best in people and situations and are generally optimistic and positive. They tend to see the opportunities that life offers, often want to try new things and are more likely to take risks. The goal of cognitive therapy is to try and change distorted thoughts (particularly negative ones) by helping people to evaluate their thinking in order to challenge their own thought processes, patterns and habits.

Over time, it was perhaps inevitable that behavioural and cognitive approaches would begin to come together. This can be seen in the work of Ellis (1962) who saw the links between emotional distress, irrational beliefs and subsequent behaviour. From this, he developed his ABCDE model:

Activating event – a negative experience (e.g. I get into trouble at school because I can't do my maths homework)

Belief system – I believe I am no good at maths, can't do it and will never be good at maths

Consequences – I start to worry about having to do any maths homework and feel sick in maths lessons

Disputing irrational beliefs – the counsellor disputes the fact that I find all maths difficult, helps me to see the aspects of maths that I can do, and emphasizes that many people experience some difficulties with maths and that everyone can learn and get better at it

Effects – this helps me to see my abilities in maths differently, shows me that I can learn too, and consequently, I start to feel better about doing maths.

Beck (1967) developed what we now know as cognitive-behavioural therapy. CBT recognizes that the way we think affects the way we feel and behave (see Figure 3.1) and is defined succinctly by Westergaard (2017: 34) as a means of 'examining the impact of negative or irrational thoughts on behaviour, and working to minimize these thoughts and change unwanted behaviours'. This process can also have a positive impact on the way people feel and subsequently cope with the challenges they face. For example, negative thinking can cause emotional distress, making people react in certain ways, such as making them argumentative, aggressive, passive or anxious. CBT challenges irrational thoughts, including the negative assumptions we make based on our previous experiences. This process of challenging thoughts and beliefs can lead to more positive experiences and emotions. Over time, beliefs and expectations can change, enabling people to change their subsequent actions and feelings.

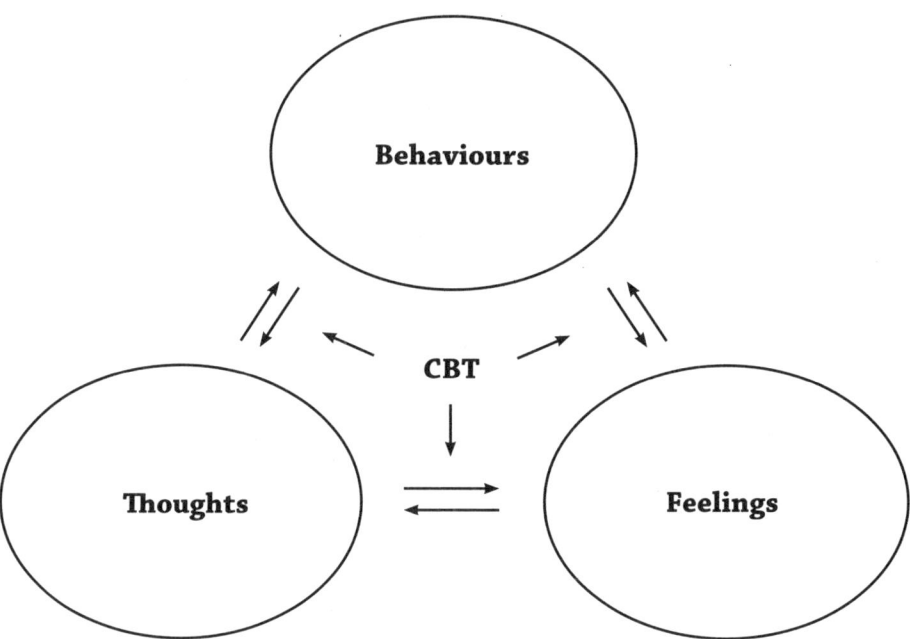

Figure 3.1 Breaking vicious cycles through CBT

CBT focuses on the present day, and helps people to set goals and thereby cope better with the things that affect their lives. Much of CBT is about helping people to break negative cycles. The theory of CBT is based on the idea of a chain of events:

- Situation: something happens (e.g. my best friend doesn't reply to my text message)
- Thoughts: the person interprets the situation (e.g. I assume I must have upset them)
- Feelings: the thoughts lead to the person experiencing an emotional and/or physical sensation (e.g. I worry about what I said in my last message and begin to feel anxious and upset because I might not have them as a friend any more)
- Behaviours: the person carries out an action in response to the emotion (e.g. I decide I no longer want them as a friend and don't contact them again).

A process of CBT helps in this situation by enabling me to change either my thoughts or my behaviour. For example, there may be a whole range of reasons why my friend hasn't contacted me. Their phone or laptop might be out of charge, or it could be broken, or have been lost or stolen. They might be too ill to contact me or have some personal difficulties that mean their time is taken up at the moment. They might be in a location with very poor internet connection. Equally, because I have known them for a long time and consider them to be my best friend, I might decide to contact them again to check that they are ok. All of this will probably make me feel better about their lack of contact and about our friendship generally. In order to make further progress, the CBT therapist sets goals and tasks for me to do in the future to enable me to make further progress, for example, when I experience or feel further rejection. Through the process of CBT, the negative cycle is broken, and distorted thinking is challenged.

Critics of CBT have argued that it is too mechanistic in its approach and fails to consider the whole person (Gaudiano, 2008). Others have described it as too simple, even simplistic. The focus of CBT is on the present and it can be criticized for failing to take past experiences into account, which might indicate some of the causes of the difficulties being experienced. Programmes of CBT are often brief (for example, six to twenty sessions), and their lasting effectiveness is sometimes questioned. Neenan and Dryden (2021) usefully discuss these criticisms and offer some counter-arguments.

CBT is now a mainstream treatment in mental health and there is some solid evidence for its effectiveness.

Step 1 — A short summary

Now write a short summary of cognitive-behavioural approaches by listing five key points:

1

2

3

4

5

Summarize why you feel it might be important for you as a social worker to have an understanding of cognitive-behavioural approaches.

Step 2 — Applying cognitive-behavioural approaches to yourself

Now try using Ellis' ABCDE model in relation to a negative experience you have had recently. Write some notes under each of the headings.

Activating event – *describe the negative experience*

Belief system – *how did this affect your belief system?*

Consequences – *what consequences did this have?*

Disputing irrational beliefs – *how would you dispute your irrational beliefs?*

Effects – *what effects did this have?*

Now choose a different negative experience and reflect on the chain of events that took place.

Situation: *what happened?*

Thoughts: *how did you interpret the situation?*

Feelings: *how did you feel?*

Behaviours: *what did you do next?*

Now think about how you could challenge your thoughts by examining some alternative reasons for what happened. What goals and tasks could you set for yourself to help you in the future?

How might all of this change your behaviour and feelings?

 **Step 3** # A case study from social work practice to illustrate cognitive-behavioural approaches

Chloe (27) has recently been offered a place on an Access course and aspires to go to university to study nursing. Chloe had a difficult upbringing; she had a poor relationship with her mother and went to live with her aunt when she was 16 following the breakdown of family relationships. Chloe has recently completed her GCSEs as a mature student and now has caring responsibilities for her grandmother, visiting her every day to help with meals. She has a strained relationship with her parents and has limited contact with them. She works part-time as an Activities Co-ordinator in a local nursing home.

Throughout her adolescence and into her adult life, Chloe has experienced depression and anxiety; she takes medication and accesses occasional support from her GP when her mood is particularly low. She had counselling as a young person, which she did not find particularly useful. In her teenage years, Chloe used self-harm as a way of managing her emotions and developed anorexia, which required a six-month inpatient stay. Chloe now describes herself as 'mainly' recovered from her eating disorder, recognizing that food can still be a source of anxiety.

Chloe has recently been referred to your service after visiting her GP to ask for help with escalating feelings of worthlessness, worry and difficulty sleeping. She tells you that she is delighted to have received an offer to study on an Access course but is concerned that she may not cope with the demands of the course saying, 'I've never been clever … I want to be a nurse because I love caring for people, but I probably won't even make it through the first year, I always seem to mess things up.' Chloe describes waking up before 6.00 am most mornings due to overwhelming feelings of stress, which she finds difficult to manage. She has a long-term partner of three years, but she lives alone because she is worried that her issues with anxiety would impact upon the relationship.

 **Step 4**   **How some knowledge of cognitive-behavioural approaches can help you to understand more about Chloe's case**

How can Chloe's case be analysed by applying the ABCDE model?

Activating event

Chloe seems to have had lots of negative experiences in her past. Perhaps the most significant of these is the breakdown of her relationship with her mother and subsequently both of her parents. This might have been because they could not cope with Chloe's self-harming and anorexia, but there could have been other reasons too that we don't know about. The current activating event seems to be the offer of a place on the Access course, which overall Chloe says she is happy about.

Belief system

Chloe is clearly experiencing a lot of self-doubt, and this has made her very anxious about how she will cope on the course. She lacks confidence in herself and in her abilities and expresses feelings of worthlessness. She believes she will fail the course, because as far as she is concerned, she has always failed in the past.

Consequences

Chloe has started waking up every day at 6.00 am. She is extremely anxious and feels unable to cope.

Disputing irrational beliefs

Chloe's irrational beliefs can be disputed in several ways and many of these involve helping her to see how much she has achieved, despite her extremely difficult circumstances. First, and very significantly, she passed her GCSEs. She achieved this while caring for her grandmother and holding down the part-time job in a local nursing home, which is no mean feat. She has also been offered a place on the Access course, which probably involved an interview and perhaps taking entrance tests as well, which is another significant achievement. It is important that Chloe understands that Access course tutors want the very best for their students and that if they felt she could not cope with the demands of the course, they would not have offered her a place, because they do not set students up to fail. It is also worth making sure that Chloe is aware of the kind of study and personal support she will receive on the Access course from the tutors and other college staff. Chloe's work experience and her love of caring for people are real assets for any future nurse. She will also be able to use her difficult life experiences when working with people in similar situations in the future.

Effects

All of this could help Chloe to see how much she has achieved so far and could help her to feel less anxious.

How can cycles of negative thinking be applied to Chloe's case?

Situation

Chloe has experienced many negative situations in her life as already discussed.

Thoughts

Chloe is thinking very negatively about her future. She feels she has always made a mess of everything in the past, and this time it will not be any different. Her negative thoughts are making her doubt her ability to cope with the Access course and in relation to the future more generally. She is assuming she will fail the course, which might mean that she is in danger of turning the place down.

Feelings

Chloe feels anxious and stressed. She feels inadequate in relation to the Access course and the nursing degree that hopefully will follow it. She feels worthless and runs herself down by describing herself as being not very clever.

Behaviours

Chloe is having difficulty sleeping and wakes very early each morning. Food can also still act as a trigger for her, but we don't know if that is the case at the moment. She is unable to live with her partner because she is worried about the impact her anxiety would have on their relationship, assuming this would be negative.

Goals and tasks

Setting goals with specific tasks could help Chloe to see more of the positives in her situation. Asking her to reflect on how she felt when she passed her GCSEs and when she was offered a place on the Access course could help her to focus on the positives in her situation. She could write her responses down and read them when she feels particularly anxious. She could also take a copy of her GCSE certificates and carry those in her bag, so she can look at them when she feels pessimistic about her studies on the Access course. Regular contact with her personal tutor is likely to be extremely helpful for Chloe, so asking her to make contact with them as soon as the course starts (or even before then if she can) would be a good task to set. Keeping in regular touch with them would be a very useful goal.

How might this change Chloe's behaviour and feelings?

All of this could reduce Chloe's levels of anxiety and help her to feel more positively about herself and the course. It is also worth assuring her that Access course tutors work with lots of students like Chloe and will do all they can to support her. She will hopefully make some good friends on the course too for mutual support, and through this, she will understand that she is not the only one that faces struggles like these and perhaps most importantly, that she isn't alone.

Step 5: Applying cognitive-behavioural approaches to your experiences in the workplace

Think about an experience you have had in the workplace where cognitive-behavioural approaches could provide some helpful explanations. Here are some questions you could ask, with space for your responses below.

Describe the experience using the ABCDE model

Now write some notes about the cycle of negative thinking the individual seems to show

What goals and tasks could you set to challenge their negative thinking?

CHAPTER 4

Solution-focused approaches

A summary

Solution-focused approaches are commonly referred to as solution-focused brief therapy (SFBT), where the emphasis is on the words 'solution' and 'brief'. SFBT developed from brief family therapy (de Shazer, 1985) and focuses on individuals finding their own solutions to the problems and issues they are facing with the support of a therapist or social worker. Sessions of SFBT typically only last for a period of six to twelve weeks. The focus is on the person's future and involves setting goals to help them solve their problems. It is all about helping them to remain (or become more) positive, and to look forward beyond the things they are experiencing at the moment. Unlike other approaches discussed so far, there is little or no interest in the past and what brought the individual to their current position. Instead, the emphasis is on looking forward. At its roots, SFBT also draws on aspects of positive psychology (see Chapter 6).

SFBT is all about working towards change and argues that individuals themselves have the skills and capacity to overcome or resolve their own difficulties. Goal setting is a particularly important part of the process as a means of helping people to select tasks that are achievable, which help them to overcome whatever issues they are currently facing and thereby make progress towards change. Goals must not be too big, and it is the individual who sets them with the help of the person supporting them. These goals help the individual to take steps forward, which can be small or even very small. Again, this is for the individual to decide for themselves, as they know what they can realistically achieve at any given point in time.

Setting achievable goals can be aided by a process of scaling. Here, people are asked to rate their difficulties at any particular time on a scale of 0 to 10, where 0 describes the problem at its worst and 10 where it has been solved. For example, if someone describes their problem as a 3 on the scale, the therapist or social worker can then ask them to set small tasks they might be able to do, to change the score to a 4 or a 5 in order to make progress towards their goal.

SFBT accepts that a small change in one part of the system can bring about change in another, and that there is no single way of resolving an issue or difficulty. Throughout the process, the individual is encouraged to focus on what is possible and what they can change, rather than being weighed down by things that they feel are impossible and will never be different.

SFBT is focused on the here and now and the therapist or social worker will often use compliments to encourage the person they are working with to be positive and to make more progress. For example, praising someone for how well they are coping at this point despite their circumstances helps them to feel they can cope and is likely to encourage them to want to do more. Equally, asking someone to think about exceptions, or times when they do not experience the problem or difficulty, is also very affirming. For example, discussing how they managed to experience those moments when things felt better (even if this only lasts for a very short time) will help them to understand more about any coping mechanisms they have developed so they can use them again in the future. All of this helps them to see more of their strengths and capabilities, emphasizing that they have the ability to make progress towards change.

Effective SFBT, as its title suggests, involves helping someone to look for solutions in order to identify what is working well and to explore ways of doing more of the same. Often this means enabling them to reflect on situations and events where they did not experience the negative effects of their difficulties. This can be done by asking coping questions followed by a discussion of how they might be able to do more of this. Asking someone to articulate what was happening (what they were thinking and doing) when they felt more positive and how they were coping at that time will help them to understand more about their reactions. They can then think about how they might be able to repeat this in other situations and circumstances in the future.

In SFBT, questions are often future orientated (see Figure 4.1). This involves asking people to envision their future without the difficulties they are currently facing and discussing how they might work towards this through setting goals and tasks. The most well-known example of a future-orientated question is a hypothetical one termed 'the miracle question'. This is where the individual is asked to imagine they wake up one morning and during the night while they have been asleep, a miracle has happened, and their problem or difficulty has completely disappeared. They are then asked to describe what would be different about their lives that would tell them that the miracle has happened. This asks them to imagine their life without the problem in specific and concrete terms and can particularly help those who feel trapped or stuck in their current situation and who feel that progress is unachievable or even impossible. The more concrete and detailed the description, the easier it will be for the person to identify tasks they can complete and goals they can set.

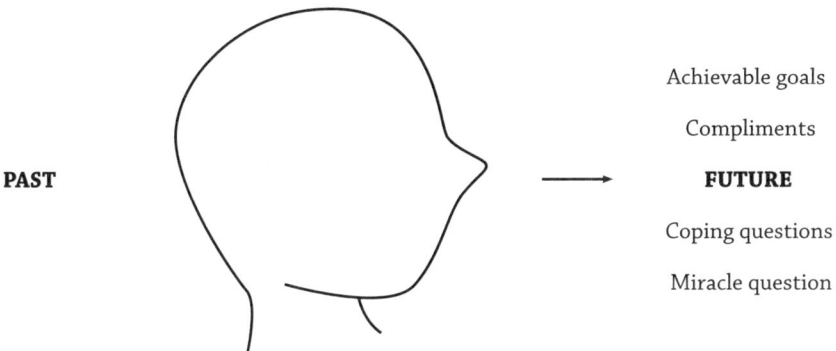

Figure 4.1 Elements of SFBT

Criticisms of SFBT tend to focus on two particular aspects that are closely linked. The first is its lack of attention to people's past experiences, which means that important emotional events can be overlooked or even ignored (Kondrat and Miller, 2020). These could provide helpful insights into an individual's thoughts, motivations and behaviours. This links with the second aspect: the brief nature of SFBT. Discussing emotions takes time and requires trust and a high level of empathy on the part of the practitioner. This also takes time to build, and time is something that SFBT practitioners simply don't have because of its quick, goal-orientated nature. The process may well not allow the practitioner sufficient time to empathize with the person they are supporting. As a result, the individual might feel misunderstood because the practitioner is not meeting them on their emotional level. Walker et al. (2022) also point out that discussing emotions can be a helpful mechanism for prompting personal change and, as such, SFBT misses this important opportunity.

SFBT is often used to help people with a range of mental health issues such as personal and work-related stress, anxiety, low self-esteem and relationship difficulties. It is most effective in situations where an individual wants to work on specific difficulties or overcome particular problems.

 **A short summary**

Now write a short summary of SFBT by listing five key points:

1

2

3

4

5

Summarize why you feel it might be important for you as a social worker to have an understanding of SFBT.

 **Step 2** Applying solution-focused approaches to yourself

Think about a problem you are currently experiencing and write some notes here.

Now try using some techniques from SFBT to describe how you might try to overcome the problem.

Write down three achievable goals that you could set to help you work towards this.

1

2

3

Think about times when the problem has not been as big as you perhaps thought. Write some notes on what helped you to feel more positive at that point.

Describe how you feel about the problem at the moment using a scale of 0–10.

What could you do to help you to move the scale towards 10?

Now ask yourself the miracle question. Imagine you wake up one morning and during the night while you have been asleep, a miracle has happened, and your problem or difficulty has completely disappeared. What would be different about your life that would tell you that the miracle has happened?

What tasks could you now complete to bring this about?

 **Step 3** — # A case study from social work practice to illustrate solution-focused approaches

You meet Kadie (31) after she has left an abusive relationship with her ex-partner, Rachel (45). Kadie is suffering from depression and anxiety.

Kadie shares that she and Rachel moved in together very quickly and were together for 'only six months'. The relationship has left a profound impact on Kadie's life. Kadie describes the way Rachel just wanted to spend time with her and not with friends and family. Kadie remembers, 'This was fine at first, as I loved being with Rachel ... my family noticed a change in me even before I did. The clothes I wore, how I acted. They were worried. I gave Rachel most of my money, as the bills were in her name. It was her flat I moved in to, I gave up my own flat. Rachel bought all the food and paid for drinks when we went out, so I didn't need much of my own money. I didn't think much of it at the time.'

Kadie says she is currently suspended from her job as a legal assistant after an anonymous complaint was made for breaching confidentiality. Kadie suspects that the complaint was made by Rachel, as Rachel was 'the only one who knew the details', but Rachel has denied this. Kadie becomes tearful and says, 'Lots of things happened in those few months. I went from being this independent woman to someone with no home, no job, no money and not even my own clothes, in a matter of months. I can't believe it has happened to me. It was all too much. Too intense. I said I was leaving for a bit and that's when she became aggressive. She threatened herself and then me with a kitchen knife. I managed to get out of the house and went straight to my mum's. Mum told me to call the police, but I couldn't, so my mum did. I feel like I've lost everything. I feel so low and depressed. I don't know who I am any more.'

Step 4 — How some knowledge of solution-focused approaches can help you to understand more about Kadie's case

Kadie appears overwhelmed by her current situation and analysing it using solution-focused approaches could help you to understand more about her case and how she can be supported.

How might Kadie be encouraged to set some goals?

Setting some achievable goals could help Kadie to make progress towards solving some of her difficulties. She is clearly very anxious about being suspended from work and she could benefit from getting some legal advice. This should be available from a local citizen's advice bureau and making an appointment to speak to someone as soon as she can could be a task that she could set. In the circumstances, there might be someone there who could speak to her employer and advocate on her behalf.

Kadie fled from a volatile and violent situation, and it seems fair to assume that all of her belongings are still in Rachel's flat. Another goal could be that she asks someone to retrieve her belongings for her. This could be her mum with the support of other family members or close friends that she trusts. It could happen at a time when she knows that Rachel will be away from the flat.

We don't know how Kadie has been paying her rent and bills to Rachel. If this is by direct debit to Rachel, another goal would be to cancel these as soon as possible.

How might using the technique of scaling help Kadie?

If Kadie scales her current difficulties from 0–10, the scores she gives are likely to be very low. Some of the achievable goals set above could help her to increase her scores. Bearing in mind how low and depressed Kadie feels, she might also set some goals aimed at trying to take some small steps towards increasing her sense of wellbeing. This could include being sure to eat well, to get some exercise (outside if she can) and taking specific time to rest and relax. All of this must come from Kadie herself as she knows what helps her the most.

How might using compliments help to support Kadie?

SFBT keeps Kadie focused on the present and not on the past. She clearly feels extremely anxious about her current situation and appears somewhat defeated by it. Complimenting her on what she has achieved so far could be an extremely helpful starting point. She has left Rachel, which is a brave and an extremely positive thing to do, particularly as she did this during turbulent and violent circumstances. Currently, she is no longer with Rachel, and she can gain some encouragement from the fact that this means she is no longer under Rachel's coercive control. Kadie can and should be praised for leaving Rachel because this represents a huge step forward in her progress towards a solution.

There are other compliments that can be given to Kadie. She immediately sought refuge with her mum who she must have stayed relatively close to during this difficult time. She knew her family were worried about her situation and perhaps even that they disapproved of her being controlled by Rachel. Even so, when things became really bad, Kadie knew what to do and where to go. She thought clearly and acted decisively to protect herself. She subsequently allowed her mum to contact the police which was another positive step. It might have been much easier for Kadie to try to persuade her mum not to do this, especially in the light of how scared she must have felt at the time, but she didn't. It seems fair to assume that Kadie probably understood what some of the consequences of this would be, bearing in mind her work in the legal field.

How might thinking of exceptions help Kadie?

Thinking about exceptions might be difficult for Kadie at the moment, but she might be able to identify some fleeting moments when she feels better now than when she first went to her mum's. There may be times when she feels less weighed down by her circumstances, and she may at times feel a sense of relief because she is no longer with Rachel.

What might Kadie's miracle question be?

If Kadie were asked the miracle question, she might respond by saying that she would have her old job back or have another enjoyable job where she can earn enough so she can live comfortably. She might talk of having her own place again, which might be far away in a place she loves where she knows Rachel can't find her. She might describe starting a new life where she is free and independent again.

Step 5: Applying solution-focused approaches to your experiences in the workplace

Think about an experience you have had in the workplace where SFBT could provide some helpful explanations. Here are some questions you could ask, with space for your responses below.

Describe the experience

List some achievable goals that you could help the individual to set

How would you use scaling to help them?

What exceptions might they be able to identify?

What compliments could you make to show them how well they are coping at the moment?

If you used the miracle question, how might they respond?

CHAPTER 5

Motivational interviewing (MI)

A summary

Motivational interviewing (MI) is a technique based in humanistic counselling (Rogers, 1959) that helps people to become more motivated for change. Many people find change difficult for a whole range of reasons and MI helps individuals to work on reducing their resistance to change and to talk in more positive terms about it. This, in turn, can lead to behavioural change. Many of the core interpersonal skills involved in MI are included in modules in social work training and are discussed in recommended texts (e.g. Loughran, 2019; Beesley et al., 2018).

MI was initially developed by Miller and Rollnick in the 1980s as a means of supporting people suffering from the effects of addiction. Since then, it has been applied much more widely in areas such as public health, criminal justice, education and of course social work. In their latest work, Miller and Rollnick (2013) describe their approach as being focused on goals that help to strengthen people's personal motivation for change and their commitment to it. This is done by exploring the individual's own reasons for change and is done in an atmosphere of acceptance and compassion.

MI was developed from the work of Prochaska and DiClemente (1983) who also did their research in the area of addiction. Their work is frequently referred to as a transtheoretical model because it draws on a number of different theoretical approaches from psychotherapy. They studied people who were trying to give up smoking without any professional support, and since then, their work has been modified to identify six stages that people go through as part of the process of change (as shown in Figure 5.1). Interestingly, and somewhat unusually, these include times when change is unlikely to happen, which are particularly worth noting. The six stages are:

1. Pre-contemplation – the person is not considering change and is probably unaware of the need for it. They think change is too difficult and they aren't ready for it.

2. Contemplation – they are beginning to get ready for change, and the balance between the pros and cons for it is fairly even. This causes a degree of ambivalence, which can lead to procrastination.
3. Preparation – the person is now ready for change and will start to take action soon. They might tell their friends and family about what they are proposing to do, and they often experience a fear of failure at this point.
4. Action – at this point, the person is fully engaged in the process of change and is working hard to continue their new behaviours.
5. Maintenance – behaviour change is now becoming embedded, but the person is still learning about those situations that can tempt them back into their old habits.
6. Termination – the change process is now complete and new behaviours are rooted in all aspects of their everyday life.

Although the stages are presented as a sequence, many people travel back and forth through them, often as a result of 'slipping back' into old habits. In addition, not everyone reaches the Termination stage, but some experience a different sixth stage called Relapse as they go back to their former ways.

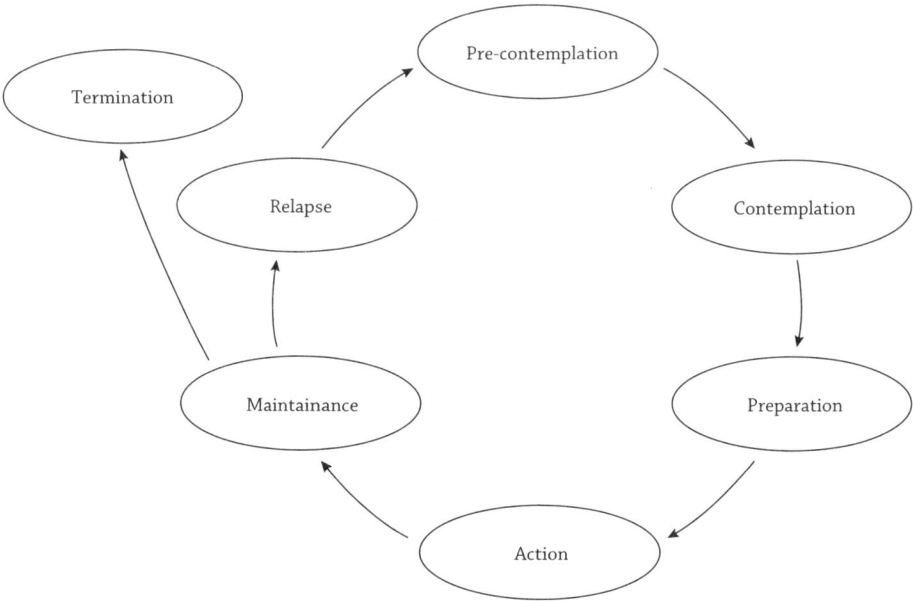

Figure 5.1 A cycle of change

Four assumptions underpin MI.
- Partnership – it is a collaborative process where the individual and practitioner work together to help the person achieve change.
- Acceptance – the practitioner is non-judgemental in their approach and seeks to understand the individual's perspectives and experiences. In addition, they respect their right to make their own decisions, including their freedom to decide not to change.
- Evocation – the client is seen as the expert on their own life. They know what they can do and when, how much or how little, what works for them and what doesn't. The practitioner enables them to see themselves better in order to identify areas where change can happen. They evoke commitment to change on the part of the client by setting goals and tasks.
- Compassion – the practitioner actively promotes and prioritizes the client's welfare and wellbeing. They have the good of the person they are supporting at heart.

MI has four key principles that can easily be remembered as EE, RR, DD and SS. They are:

a) Expressing empathy (EE) – as human beings, most of us have the ability to understand and share the feelings of others. This is empathy and in MI, the practitioner expresses this to show the client they appreciate their situation and the difficulties this brings.

b) Rolling with resistance (RR) – many people resist change for reasons that are very real to them, even when they can see the damage their current situation is doing to their lives. In MI, the practitioner helps to divert the individual's negative thinking by helping them to focus on positive aspects of change.

c) Developing discrepancy (DD) – in this context, a discrepancy is an illogical or surprising difference between two or more things that an individual says. In MI, the practitioner can help the client to understand more about the ways in which their thoughts, behaviour and action (or lack of action) is at odds with what they want to achieve in the change process.

d) Supporting self-efficacy (SS) – self-efficacy is described by Bandura (1986) as an individual's judgement of their ability to carry out actions to achieve their goals. People with a high degree of self-efficacy believe in their ability to change, which is key to a successful process of MI. People need support and encouragement to develop this further.

Practitioners need a range of excellent interpersonal skills for MI to be effective. These start with listen, listen and listen some more and are easily remembered by using the acronym OARS.

Open questions – these questions cannot be answered by a simple yes or no and encourage the client to speak freely. Typically, they start with words like what, when and how.

Affirmations – the focus here is on the person's strengths and things they have achieved so far (however small). Affirmations build confidence in their ability to change and a stronger sense of hope in the future.

Reflections – sometimes called reflecting back, this is when the practitioner paraphrases what the individual has said in order to help them to see the points they are making more clearly. Importantly, it shows them that they have been heard.

Summaries – these can help to keep a conversation on track and offer both participant and practitioner time for further thought. They also give the individual the opportunity to say if the practitioner has not understood them correctly, and the chance to express themselves differently in order to be better understood.

Teater (2020) argues that MI might not be a suitable approach for every client, for example, those who find it difficult to make a link between their current behaviour and values for the future. One of the major criticisms of MI is that its effects dwindle over time and that the outcomes of some very large trials have been disappointing in this regard (Luty and Iwanowicz, 2018). A lack of good training in the MI approach is also highlighted as a weakness by some critics (Mesters, 2009). Bell and Roomaney (2020) explored some of the reasons why practitioners are reluctant to use MI and found somewhat unsurprisingly that those who were less committed to it, found it to be less effective.

MI can be useful for a number of individuals including those with a high level of ambivalence who are stuck and have very mixed feelings about change. It can also be useful when self-efficacy is low, and people have little confidence in their ability to change. They might also have little desire for change and feel that the benefits of change are unclear or too difficult to achieve in their current circumstances.

 **A short summary**

Now write a short summary of MI by listing five key points:

1

2

3

4

5

Summarize why you feel it might be important for you as a social worker to have an understanding of MI.

 **Step 2** **Applying MI to yourself**

Now think about a time when MI might have been useful for you. Describe the situation and the context.

Now describe the change process that you experienced using Prochaska and DiClemente's stages.

1. Pre-contemplation

2. Contemplation

3. Preparation

4. Action

5. Maintenance

6. Termination or Relapse

Now think about these key areas in relation to your change process.

Evocation – *what would have helped you to understand more about yourself?*

Rolling with resistance – *what was stopping you from engaging with the process of change and how did you overcome this? If you feel you didn't overcome it, what got in the way?*

Discrepancies – *describe some of them here.*

Self-efficacy – *how has this developed through this experience and which areas do you feel you still need to work on?*

Step 3 A case study from social work practice to illustrate MI

Peggy is a 64-year-old woman with some significant physical health problems, including high blood pressure, Type 2 diabetes and osteoarthritis. Peggy is significantly overweight, and many of her health problems are exacerbated by obesity. Until five years ago, Peggy lived with her mother and was very close to her; however, Peggy's mother died after a long illness and Peggy was left to live alone in the ground-floor flat which they previously shared.

Last year, Peggy was diagnosed with breast cancer and is in remission following treatment. Peggy uses a mobility scooter to get around, although she has not left the house for some months. The district nurse contacted your service to express some worries about Peggy as she has noticed a deterioration in Peggy's mental and physical health. The nurse tells you that Peggy's home has always been quite cluttered; however, over the last few years, several rooms have become unusable as they are full of belongings from the past and new items that Peggy has bought on the internet. When you visit, you discover that Peggy has been sleeping on a chair in the living room as she cannot access her bedroom. You see that the cooker is broken, and you are concerned about the living conditions in the kitchen and bathroom.

When you share your worries with Peggy, she becomes distressed. Peggy tells you, 'When I recovered from the cancer, I felt like I had been given a second chance at life. I want to make changes, like eat healthier food and have a clear-out so that I can have my space back, but I always seem to fall back into old habits – eating too much, hiding myself away. I feel like my life is over, what's the point of trying to do anything differently now?'

 **Step 4**   **How some knowledge of MI can help you to understand more about Peggy's case**

How can Prochaska and DiClemente's model be applied to Peggy?

Peggy seems stuck in her current situation and analysing her position using Prochaska and DiClemente's model shows that she is probably in the alternative Stage 6 Relapse, particularly because she talks about falling back into her old ways. We don't know how far she has managed to achieve change in the past, but multiple issues have given her some severe setbacks. Following her remission from cancer, she felt she wanted to change, and she was able to articulate some of the key things she needed to do but found she was simply unable to do them. To move forward, Peggy needs support in re-entering the cycle at Stage 2 Pre-contemplation in order to prepare for change.

Which of the four assumptions underpinning MI apply to Peggy?

Partnership

Working effectively with Peggy will mean establishing and developing a close partnership with her. Currently Peggy is very alone, she is still grieving the loss of her mother and needs to work with someone to help her try and achieve change.

Acceptance

Peggy needs to experience acceptance and working with her in a non-judgemental way will be important in helping her to feel genuinely understood. Peggy must understand that she can and should make her own decisions and that whatever she decides to do, or not do, you will respect her for it.

Evocation

Peggy is the expert on her own life. She knows what she can achieve and what she can't, and what works for her and what doesn't. Peggy needs support in seeing herself more clearly so that she can pinpoint areas (however small) where she can change. She can achieve this if she has clear and achievable tasks and goals that she can set.

Compassion

Perhaps most of all, Peggy needs to experience some compassion. She needs to know that someone is interested in her, cares for her and has her wellbeing at heart.

How might the four key principles of MI be applied?

Expressing empathy (EE)

Peggy needs to hear clearly that you understand her position and can share some of her feelings. However, nobody can say that they completely understand someone else's feelings because every individual and every situation is different and thereby unique. However, we all have some things in common and it is not difficult for us to imagine how Peggy might be feeling at the moment and how we might feel in her circumstances. Peggy needs to hear that you understand and that you are on her side.

Rolling with resistance (RR)

Peggy seems to have become disillusioned with the prospect of being able to change. She felt much more positive when her cancer went into remission, but she has now slipped back into her old habits. She probably assumes that change will just be too difficult to achieve, even though she knows her current lifestyle is causing her damage. Peggy needs help in diverting her negative thinking so that she can focus on positive aspects of change.

Developing discrepancy (DD)

There are some discrepancies in what Peggy says, in that she can see that her remission from cancer has given her a second chance. She also understands some of the key changes she needs to make to make her life better. These include eating more healthily, which would help her to tackle her obesity, and clearing her cluttered flat. However, she says she is unable to do this.

Supporting self-efficacy (SS)

At the moment, Peggy does not believe she is able to change and doesn't see the point in trying to change now. Her level of self-efficacy is very low, and she needs help and support to strengthen this.

How might you listen to Peggy?

Listening to Peggy will be especially important, particularly as she spends much of her time alone. It will involve helping her to speak freely using particular techniques.

- **O**pen questions – asking Peggy questions starting with what, when and how will help her speak freely.
- **A**ffirmations – Peggy will probably struggle to see her strengths. However, she cared for her mother through a long illness, and not everyone can do this. She

has also reached the point where her cancer is in remission, which also takes courage. Affirming these achievements will help to build Peggy's confidence and give her a stronger sense of her ability to cope. It could also give her more hope for her future.

Reflections – as Peggy articulates her circumstances and her achievements, it will be important to reflect these back to her because this will reinforce what she is saying. This will help her to know that you have listened and that she has been heard.

Summaries – these will help to keep the conversation on track and to keep things focused on the future. They give you and Peggy time for further thought and give you the opportunity to emphasize to Peggy what she has achieved so far, however little this might be. There may be times when Peggy needs to adjust what you are saying in the light of a summary. This all helps Peggy to understand herself better and helps you to understand her better too.

 **Step 5**   Applying MI to your experiences in the workplace

Think about an experience you have had in the workplace where MI could provide some helpful explanations. Here are some questions you could ask, with space for your responses below.

Describe the experience and the context

Now describe the change process that the individual experienced using Prochaska and DiClemente's stages.

1   Pre-contemplation

2   Contemplation

3   Preparation

4   Action

5   Maintenance

6   Termination or Relapse

Now think about these key areas in relation to the individual's change process.

Evocation – *what would have helped them to understand more about themselves?*

Rolling with resistance – *what was stopping them from engaging with the process of change and how did they try to overcome this? If they didn't overcome it, what got in the way?*

Discrepancies – *describe some of them here.*

Self-efficacy – *how has the person developed this and which areas do you feel they still need to work on?*

What have you learned from this experience about your interpersonal skills?

How can you continue to develop your interpersonal skills to help you use MI effectively with the people you are supporting?

CHAPTER 6

Strengths-based perspectives

A summary

Until relatively recent times, many theories and models used in social work focused primarily on the problems and difficulties faced by individuals. This often served to cast the person being supported in the role of victim and was demoralizing for social workers (Howe, 2009). In short, it was often felt that people's lives would be better if their circumstances were somehow improved. However, neoliberal individualized ideologies placed the responsibility for this firmly on the individual, who needed to do all they could to make their circumstances better. These theoretical approaches are termed deficit models and social work was not alone in having these as its focus. It also applied to others in professions such as teaching and career guidance. Whether it was working harder to improve your grades or 'getting on your bike' to find a job (a famous speech given by Norman Tebbit at the Tory party conference in 1981 at a time of high unemployment), the onus was on the individual to do all they could to improve their own circumstances. Such deficit models still exist today. This book was written as the UK began to live with Covid-19, the war in Ukraine continued, a cost-of-living crisis bit hard, and energy prices soared. The media was full of tips to help people save money, while energy companies continued to make enormous profits.

In the late twentieth and early twenty-first century, strengths-based perspectives began to turn some of this deficit thinking on its head and these were a dramatic departure from conventional social work theory and practice. These perspectives are based in positive psychology (Seligman and Csikszentmihályi, 2000). The foundations for positive psychology were laid by Seligman and Maier's research in the 1960s and 1970s which identified the phenomenon of 'learned helplessness'. At the time, they asserted that in general people do not try to get out of difficult situations because the past has taught them that they are helpless in these situations. Like Pavlov (1928), Seligman and Maier's (1967) studies were carried out with dogs. Much later, the concept of 'learned helplessness' was modified by Maier and Seligman (2016) following discoveries in neuroscience which have confirmed that passivity (or helplessness) is not learned, but is the automatic default response to prolonged adverse events. Thankfully humans can learn to overcome automatic passivity by developing control.

Strengths-based perspectives involve forward thinking, focusing on all future possibilities, and in particular on what the person can control. The emphasis has moved from 'learned helplessness' to 'learned optimism' (Seligman, 1991) which recognizes people's resilience and resourcefulness. Resilience is often defined as a person's capacity to bounce back and adapt in the face of adversity (Higgins, 1994). In addition, people have resources at their disposal to help them to achieve this, in particular, the relationships they build with people around them. In short, people are much more than their problem, issue or circumstances.

Six practice principles for strengths-based approaches were developed by Kisthardt (2013) (as shown in Figure 6.1) and they are as follows:

1. Take an optimistic stance – focus on the individual's strengths, desires, interests and hopes, not on their problems, issues and circumstances.
2. All human beings have the capacity to learn – we all have some resilience, and it can grow and develop in the light of the experiences we have.
3. People have the right to try, succeed, to make mistakes and to learn from all of this.
4. Collaboration is the basis for the working relationship – this work is best done in partnership with the person.
5. Work in familiar surroundings – working with people in their community settings is preferable because they provide protection for individuals and help to minimize risk.
6. Community as a resource – local communities and the people within them are an enormous resource and involving them will help people to tap into the support available.

Using a strengths-based approach means focusing on whatever is working well (however small this might be) and helping the individual to see how they can do more of the same. This means giving people opportunities to discuss their strengths, abilities, talents, interests and skills. This is often done well by encouraging the person to tell their story. Most people find it relatively easy to talk about themselves and their experience and are keen for (and might even long for) someone to listen.

These approaches highlight the need for people to have supportive relationships. They will be able to achieve much more with others around them than on their own. If such support comes from their local community (including

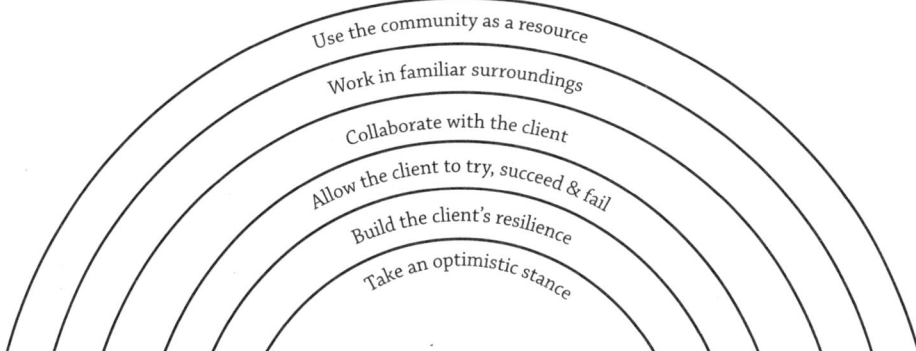

Figure 6.1 Six practice principles for a strengths-based approach

family and friends), it will be much more readily available than the support of professionals and will be easier to access. However, support from professionals is very important in helping the individual see themselves more clearly, where their support mechanisms are and how they might access them to best effect. Working well with people using a strengths-based approach means being genuinely interested in and respectful of their stories, narratives and accounts. It also means believing that the individual is the expert on their own lives and that they have the capacity to overcome their difficulties.

Saleebey has written extensively on the application of the strengths-based approach in social work and highlights some of the major general criticisms of it, for example those who say it is simply about 'uplifting mantras', the power of positive thinking or 'ignoring reality' (Saleebey, 1996: 302). Gray (2011: 8) argues that in spite of using 'the language of social justice and empowerment', the solutions that the approach suggests are 'essentially grounded in (neo)liberal notions of individual responsibility'. She argues that it adopts the theory of community development uncritically, claiming 'to take structural considerations into account' when these are not the main focus of the approach.

Saleebey (2002) identifies a number of types of questions that can be used effectively in a strengths-based approach. These include

- Survival questions – asking who has helped in the past and how they did this. How was contact made and what kind of support were they able to give?
- Exception questions – discussing what was happening when times were better and what was working well. What were they doing then that made things improve?

- Possibility questions – focusing on hope and how they might be able to move forward to bring about a more hopeful perspective.
- Esteem questions – helping someone to articulate their strengths, abilities and talents. This is often easier if it is phrased in such a way where the emphasis is on what others would say rather than what they would say themselves, for example, asking how a close relative or best friend would describe their strengths.

Finally, giving compliments is important too. People need encouragement to keep going and telling them how well they are doing, especially with some specific examples (however small) where possible, will keep them moving forward.

Step 1 A short summary

Now write a short summary of strengths-based perspectives by listing five key points:

1

2

3

4

5

Summarize why you feel it might be important for you as a social worker to have an understanding of strengths-based perspectives.

 **Step 2** Applying strengths-based perspectives to yourself

Has your life been affected by deficit models in any way? If so, how and if not, why not?

Describe your own level of resilience.

How might you be able to develop more of this?

What resources do you have in your own community of people?

Now write under each of these questions.
- **Survival questions** – *who has helped you in the past and how did they do this? How did you make contact with these people and what kind of support were they able to give you?*

- **Exception questions** – *what was happening when times were better for you and what was working well? What were you doing then that made things improve?*

- **Possibility questions** – *what do you hope for in the future? How might you be able to move forward to bring about a more hopeful perspective?*

- **Esteem question** – *write about your strengths, abilities and talents. If you don't find this easy, think about how your best friend or someone close to you might describe you. Remember to focus only on positives.*

A case study from social work practice to illustrate strengths-based perspectives

James (25) was released from prison five months ago and is residing in supported accommodation, awaiting allocation of his own property. James has a long history of criminal activity, including theft and burglary, and tells you that he turned to crime primarily to fund his substance misuse, which 'got out of hand'. James shared that he used heroin and cocaine every day before his prison sentence. He was sentenced to six months in prison and served three months. James states he is now 'clean' and is prescribed methadone. He adds, 'I needed prison to kick me into touch'. James has been working with a substance misuse service since his release, and they report he engages well and has not missed an appointment yet. The service is planning to reduce James' methadone in the next few weeks.

James tells you he has a 3-year-old daughter, Isabel, who he has not seen since she was a young baby. He says, 'Isabel's mum won't let me near her until I get my own place and can prove I'm doing ok. She doesn't trust me'. James has a difficult relationship with his family and tells you, 'I've stolen from my mum and my auntie. They always tried to help me in the past, but when I stole from them, it all changed. All my family ended contact when I went to prison. I don't blame them, but I'd like them to see I'm trying to change now'. James tells you that he started college to become a builder when he was 18 years old and wishes he had stuck to this plan. James shared that he 'got in with a bad crowd and just quit college after a few months'. James would like to be in employment or study going forward. He states, 'I know it will be hard. Who wants someone like me working for them? I just want a chance to prove I can do it and show everyone I can move forward'. James feels isolated where he is living, adding 'It's not an area I know. Plus, there's loads of drug users around here and it's so hard to stay on track. I need my own place'.

Step 4 — How some knowledge of strengths-based perspectives can help you to understand more about James' case

How has James' life been affected by deficit models?

James has a long history of criminal activity to fund his substance misuse and this resulted in time in prison. Deficit models would argue that it is now up to James to turn his life around. His daughter's mum doesn't trust him and will only allow him to see her when he can show that he has done this successfully. He has no contact with the rest of his family after he stole from them. If he is to have fresh contact with them, they would probably expect him to change too.

How can you take an optimistic stance with James?

This means focusing on James' strengths, desires, interests and hopes and not on his problems and issues. James has responsibility for his own life and has the capacity to learn and change. But he can only change things that he can control, and he will need some help to identify these. He shows some resilience and working in partnership with him will help him to develop more. He needs to build and extend his community in order to access more resources that can support him.

A good starting point is to ask James what he feels is working well at the moment, which will also involve giving him compliments. He has been out of prison for five months and has stayed clean during this time, despite living in an area where there are lots of drug users. Having used heroin and cocaine every day in the past, this is a real achievement. He only served three months of his six-month sentence, which shows that he must have made very good progress while in custody. He has been engaging well with the substance misuse service and his methadone prescription will be reduced soon, which shows he is still progressing well. These are all very positive things that James can be complimented on and that show he has developed some resilience.

James needs to focus on his strengths, talents, interests and skills. He seems to have enjoyed his college course and regrets leaving. This suggests that he has some practical interests and skills. He has some clear hopes for the future; in particular, he wants to be able to see his daughter and to start to build a relationship with her. He would like a job or to study to help him to move forward towards this. He would also like to have contact with his family again. He wants his own place away from the influence of drug users.

What is the role of the community in James' case?

James says he feels isolated, so he needs support in building his community. A good starting point is the supported accommodation and the substance misuse service where he might be able to access further support, particularly in relation to employment and training. They might be able to introduce James to people in local organizations, such as colleges and training providers who run courses for offenders as well as providing them with mentors and role models. In addition, there might be other charitable organizations in the area involved in social prescribing that could reach out to James.

What kinds of questions could you ask James?

Using a strengths-based approach, you could ask James

- Survival questions such as who has helped him in the past (for example, when he first came out of prison) and how they did this. How did he make contact with these people and what kind of support were they able to give him?
- Exception questions such as what was happening when times were better for him and what was working well. What was he doing then that made things improve?
- Possibility questions that focus on what he hopes for in the future and how he might be able to move forward to bring about a more hopeful perspective.
- Esteem questions about his strengths, abilities and talents. Remember, if he doesn't find this easy, he could think about what a good friend, or someone working in the substance misuse service would say about him.

Step 5: Applying strengths-based perspectives to your experiences in the workplace

Think about an experience you have had in the workplace where a strengths-based approach could provide some helpful explanations. Here are some questions you could ask, with space for your responses below.

How has the person's life been affected by deficit models?

Describe their level of resilience.

How might they be able to develop in this area?

What resources do they have in their community of people?

Now write some questions that you could ask them under these headings:

○ Survival questions

○ Exception questions

○ Possibility questions

○ Esteem questions

CHAPTER 7

Systems theory

A summary

So far in this book, we have concentrated on theoretical approaches that have the individual at their centre. In the next four chapters, the focus shifts to theories that give a central position to society more broadly. Many of these argue that looking at the individual's position alone is not enough when trying to understand their difficulties and issues. We all live in a social context, and this affects how we experience our everyday lives. Many people face economic and personal challenges that can be better understood by examining issues of context. At the time of writing, this was particularly clear as we were all living with a cost-of-living crisis and even people who would not usually struggle with heating their homes were faced with a choice between eating and heating.

This chapter focuses on systems theory, which argues that everything in society is connected. In short, every action we take affects something else and can change it, for better or for worse. We see this perhaps most starkly in relation to climate change. People in the developed and developing world continue to use fossil fuels that raise temperatures around the globe. As a result, ice caps keep melting, and the implications are evident as wildlife habitats disappear and low-lying countries around the world potentially face devastation through rising sea levels. Many others suffer too because of extreme weather conditions such as droughts, floods and hurricanes that have disastrous consequences. What happens in the polar ice caps has an effect all over the world – everything is linked together.

Systems theory argues that we can't understand the whole without looking at the parts, and we can't understand the parts without looking at the whole. One of the difficulties of looking at systems in general is the enormity and complexity of them. So what is a system? The human body is probably one of the best tangible examples of a system (Howe, 2009). Each part affects the other and a change in one part can lead to a change in another. When one part goes wrong, the effects are felt by the whole body. In systems theory terms, this is known as reciprocity.

Healy (2014) discusses three waves of systems theory:

1. General systems theory – as discussed previously, this challenged the individualistic focus of many approaches in the helping professions, including social work, and in the 1960s sought to apply biological explanations of systems to social settings (von Bertalanffy, 1968). This drew attention to the relationship between people and their environments and the transactions that accompany this. For example, people living in an area of significant deprivation experience all sorts of challenges because of the interaction they have with their context.
2. Ecosystems – this second wave began to emerge in the 1970s and used ecology (defined in biology as the relationship of organisms to one another and to their physical surroundings) as a metaphor for social work practice (Meyer, 1976). This moved systems thinking forward to consider how different systems influence and can be influenced by each other. Most people have transactions with multiple systems, for example, health care services (multiple systems in themselves), schools, local councils and community organizations. Many difficulties arise because of a poor fit between a person and their environment and also because the different systems fail to interact with each other. Health care is a good example where an individual with multiple health conditions can have a number of different specialists working on their case, which can adversely affect their care if the professionals fail to communicate with one another.
3. Complex systems – this third wave is also known as complexity theory. This is linked with developments in chaos theory which emphasize the endemic nature of constant change in and between systems. These changes are often non-linear which make them very difficult to predict. Applying this to social work theory and practice is still a work in progress.

Healy (2014) helpfully argues that systems operate at three different levels (see Figure 7.1).

1. Macro – here we think about the big picture with systems that operate at a national and even international level. The UK's NHS (National Health Service) is one example, as is the WHO (World Health Organization).
2. Meso – here we have many of the organizations and institutions people have contact with in their daily lives. Schools, colleges and prisons are all examples.
3. Micro – this is where most contact is experienced, for example, in the home and local neighbourhood.

When examining the difficulties and issues that people face, it is clear that these rarely have a single cause. Systems theory shows that we need to see things

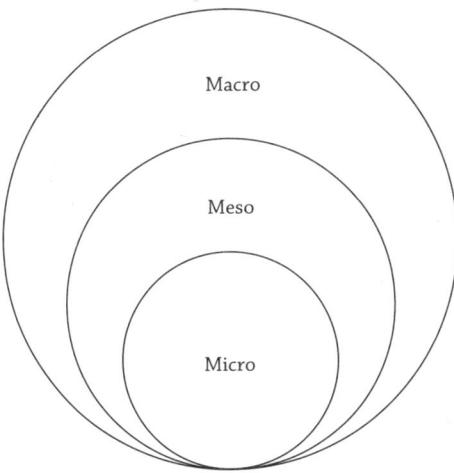

Figure 7.1 The three levels of systems theory

from different perspectives to gain greater understanding. Family therapy was an early example of systems theory at work in social work practice, and many cases show that it is important to see what is happening between people and to respond to people in their environment. Some families operate as open systems which accept feedback and work with it (Hanna, 1997). This makes them more adaptable to change. But others operate as closed systems that shut themselves off from the outside world and try to solve problems themselves from within, which can make change difficult to navigate. Systems can be described as porous; they allow flow from inside to outside and vice versa but are not thereby dissolved. Payne (2021: 233) uses the metaphor of a teabag to explain this very clearly.

One of the major criticisms of systems theory is that while it makes complexities clear, it can be difficult to use in practice and does not offer methods that can work towards achievable outcomes (Payne, 2021). Overall, it helps a practitioner to gain a greater understanding of a person's experiences by helping them to understand their context but does not give techniques that can then be used and lead to action points. Goldstein (1975:18) sums this up neatly when he states that while systems theory 'offers lucid, useful explanations of social phenomena, it does not prescribe what, specifically, one should do to remedy them'. Systems are complex and often it is very difficult to know which part or parts of a particular system need to be questioned or challenged. This again makes systems theory difficult to apply in practice. In addition, some argue that it does more to maintain the status quo by asking people to fit in with and adapt to the system they are a part of, as opposed to challenging it. Challenging large systems successfully is, of course, an extremely difficult thing to do.

Initially, systems theory led to ideas for unitary social work practice in the 1970s, but these were too difficult to implement as social workers tried to work across multiple client groups. This moved forward to interdisciplinary work, where different professionals sought to work together. This was highlighted by the development of the Connexions youth support service in the early twenty-first century. Aspects of this remain but it is now more common for specialists to work together with other professionals, which we know can be challenging for a number of reasons. Systems theory offers a way of understanding complexity and uncertainty, but in many cases, it focuses on maintaining social cohesion rather than promoting more radical social change.

 **A short summary**

Now write a short summary of systems theory by listing five key points:

1

2

3

4

5

Summarize why you feel it might be important for you as a social worker to have an understanding of systems theory.

 **Step 2** Applying systems theory to yourself

Make a list of the systems that you are part of under the following headings:

Macro

Meso

Micro

Now think of an example from your own experience where systems have worked well together. How did this happen and what brought it about?

Now think of an example from your own experience where systems did not work well together. How did this happen and how could it have been improved?

Systems theory 89

 **Step 3** # A case study from social work practice to illustrate systems theory

You have been working with Kane (15) and his family for the past month following a referral made by the police when Kane went missing overnight.

Kane lives with his father, Andrew, following a breakdown in his relationship with his mother, Anne-Marie, last year. Andrew and Anne-Marie separated when Kane was 11 years old. Anne-Marie now has two younger children with her partner, Wayne. Anne-Marie has said to you on the telephone that Kane was a 'bad influence' on her younger children and that she struggled with Kane's behaviour, stating that he had been aggressive. Anne-Marie reports that Kane will sometimes 'turn up asking for money' at her home and when this is not provided, he will 'kick off'. She tries to contact Kane by phone, but he rarely answers and if he does, she states 'He is stoned'. Kane tells you he does not go to his mum's house much any more. He states, 'They don't care about me and I don't care about them. Let them have their cosy little family'.

Andrew shares that Kane has begun staying out late and sometimes overnight with other young people in the area. He says some of these young people look 18 and 19 years old and asks you, 'What do these lads want to hang around with kids for?' Andrew is getting increasingly upset and angry that Kane won't tell him where he is or who he is with.

Kane attends a local school, but in the last few weeks he has only attended once or twice each week and has arrived smelling strongly of cannabis. Kane has a supportive learning mentor in school called Carmel. Carmel shares that Kane has always struggled academically but loves sports. He is a keen footballer. Carmel expresses her sadness that Kane doesn't go to his local football club any more and seems distant from his friends in school.

You are aware from Anne-Marie and Andrew that Kane has extended family on his maternal and paternal sides, but they have been reluctant to support Kane so far due to their own family commitments.

 **Step 4**   How some knowledge of systems theory can help you to understand more about Kane's case

Systems theory encourages us to look at Kane's case as a whole and to break it down into its constituent parts to see how they are affecting one another. In this case, you are working with the whole family.

Which systems are at play in Kane's case?

Macro – the referral to you was made by the police after Kane went missing one night.

Meso – at this level, the main system in operation is Kane's school and Carmel is a particularly important part of this. The local football club is another system, although Kane has stopped going there.

Micro – Kane's family operates at this level and is made up of his estranged parents. He also has extended family on both sides. The older young people that he mixes with locally are an example of another system as are his friends from school.

Which systems are working well and why?

These are difficult to identify. The school seems generally supportive, and Carmel has certainly had a positive relationship with Kane until relatively recently. Kane's circle of friends (those who seem older than him) is also operating well, although they seem to be having a negative influence on him and his drug misuse is a cause for concern.

Which are not working well and why?

There are several systems that are not working well for Kane. The first is his immediate family, which broke up when he was 11. Clearly, this had a big effect on him, and Kane left his mum and her partner after three years to go and live with his dad. His mum's family grew when she had two children with a new partner and Kane clearly resents this. He is probably suffering from the loss of close contact with his mum and the security that his family home gave him. The extended family members (his grandparents) no longer have any contact with Kane, so this system can be described as broken. Kane has stopped going to the football club, which means his local friendship system has broken down too. Because he only attends school a couple of days each week, this system is also partially broken.

How might systems be able to work better together to help Kane?

Systems theory shows that we need to examine Kane's case from different perspectives. In order to work better together, systems need to collaborate with each other. But this does not happen automatically and needs dedicated individuals to make this happen. As a social worker, a key aspect of your role in Kane's case is to bring the different systems together to support Kane.

First is the system of Kane's family, which has been broken for a while. There is important work here in bringing the family together to share their different perspectives on what is happening for Kane, including Kane himself. No doubt they will each have a different take on what has been happening. This work will undoubtedly involve lots of listening and some well-developed skills of diplomacy. It is important that each family member is heard and their contributions accepted and appreciated.

Second, there are some other key players who could have a positive contribution to make to this case. Carmel is part of the school system and can have an influence on devising support mechanisms within the school to try to re-ignite Kane's motivation for learning and to attend more often. She may know of key members of school staff who have a good relationship with Kane whom she can bring into the process. In her role as a learning mentor, Carmel will also have contact with people outside the school such as those working for colleges, charities and community organizations supporting young people in the area who aren't attending school. She may have contact with the football club and the local police too. In addition, there may be people in the locality working with people misusing drugs, who could be contacted for their particular expertise.

When this groundwork has been done, a plan of action will be needed to change the rhetoric into practice. Oversight of this will be a key part in keeping systems communicating with each other to bring this about. As a social worker, your role will be important in this respect, and Carmel will have an important part to play in this too.

Step 5 — Applying systems theory to your experiences in the workplace

Think about an experience you have had in the workplace where systems theory could provide some helpful explanations. Here are some questions you could ask, with space for your responses below.

Make a list of the common systems that people in the local area are part of under the following headings:

Macro

Meso

Micro

Now think of an example from your experience in the workplace where systems have worked well together. How did this happen and what brought it about?

Now think of an example from your experience in the workplace where systems did not work well together. How did this happen and how could it have been improved?

CHAPTER 8

Critical practice

A summary

While systems theory focuses on maintaining social cohesion, critical practice, with its roots in radical social work, emphasizes the need to challenge the status quo in seeking to improve the lives of those on the margins and particularly people living in poverty. The early roots of radical social work can be found as far back as the 1950s in the work of various religious groups including the Quakers. The popular TV series *Call the Midwife* set in the 1950s and 60s could be described as radical midwifery. Here the nurses and nuns work with the poorest families in the East End of London, often challenging those with power in the community on the inadequacy of local services, thereby seeking to improve the lives of people in Poplar. Unlike neoliberal individualized ideologies which place the responsibility for overcoming inequality firmly on the individual, radical social work argues that society's problems (such as poverty) are caused by people in power. As Howe (2009: 123) states forcefully, 'Being poor was not part of the natural order. It was not the result of flaws and failings. It was largely "man-made".' The way to counter this was through collective action, but this was difficult to translate into social work practice and left practitioners feeling either guilty or helpless.

Critical practice was influenced by critical theory, which aims to critique and change society as a whole. It argues that the fabric of society is socially constructed with ruling and powerful social groups being able to justify injustice and inequality through their control of language, the media, education and political debate. From this perspective, theories such as those discussed in the first half of this book, that focus on the individual, are part of the problem because they result in people themselves being said to be responsible and even to blame for their problems, which are primarily not of their making. The stance of critical theory is that we need to be critical of society and its structures (see the S in Thompson's PCS model in Chapter 10).

In more recent years, the postmodern writings of Foucault have been particularly influential in critical theory, showing how power operates within society in everyday relationships. In his book *Discipline and Punish* (Foucault,

1977), he shows how the history of the prison system in France has developed over time, not in response to the welfare of prisoners but in order to exercise power to coerce and control people. He refers back to the design of Jeremy Bentham's prison (the Panopticon) to demonstrate this. Bentham was an English philosopher and social theorist who lived during the eighteenth century, and the Panopticon was a circular building with cells on the outside wall and an inspection tower at the centre.

The prison was designed in such a way as to allow one single inspector in the tower to see into each cell through small windows without the prisoners being able to see them. This gave rise to the notion of seeing without being seen. The prisoners would never know when they were actually being watched because they couldn't see the inspector, but this meant they thought the inspector might be watching them at any moment. A number of prisons were built following this design but are no longer in use because they were thought to be inhumane. However, Foucault's arguments have been used to show how power, coercion and control are used in society through the notion of seeing without being seen. We only have to look at all the security cameras around us to be aware of the idea of being watched, even though we don't actually know whether or not a particular camera is working at that moment in time.

Critical theory (like postmodern theory) argues that there are no single grand answers to issues and problems. Truth is relative and has local explanations which result in multiple perspectives on single issues. The postmodern world is fluid, constantly changing and open to interpretation. Discourse (defined here as written or spoken communication between people) is controlled by dominant groups who hold power in society (for example, politicians), and these discourses define social relationships. Critical theory argues that unless power is examined, it remains hidden, and oppression becomes covert through the use of language, and people then start to define themselves by the dominant discourses. As Fook (2007: 368) states, 'individuals can participate in their own domination, by holding self-defeating beliefs about their place in the social structure, their own power and possibilities for change'. People start to govern themselves because they are told they should be able to cope when they can't, and they feel guilty about this. Whether this is being able to manage financially during a cost-of-living crisis, control our weight or our children, we feel the burden of responsibility for this ourselves (see Figure 8.1). So external control becomes less necessary as we are happy to comply and submit to dominant discourses.

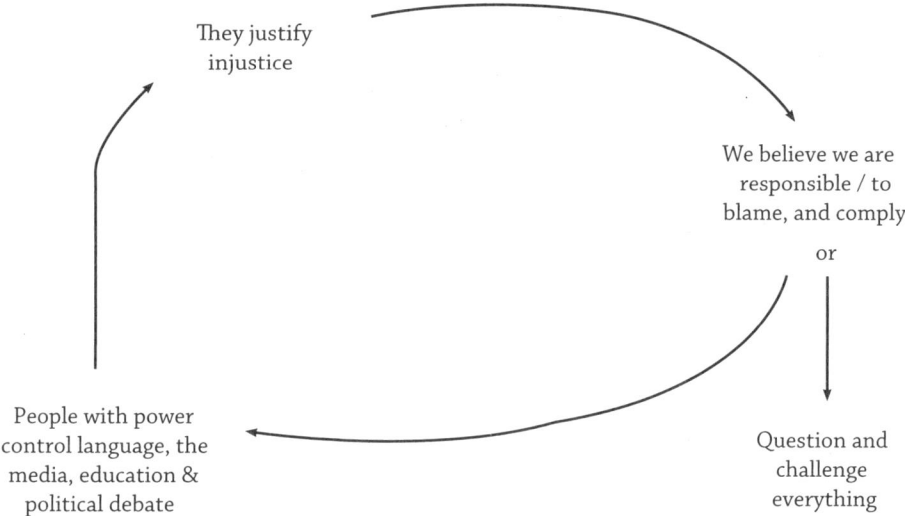

Figure 8.1 Critical practice

Critical theory argues that like the prisoners in the Panopticon, power in society is regulated from within. In fact, in the Panopticon, it is perfectly possible that there is no guard in the tower and never has been, but the prisoners believe there is, so they adapt their behaviour accordingly. This is how dominant discourses operate, where language is never neutral but always conveys meaning. For example, at the time of writing, the prime minister (Rishi Sunak) invited trade unions to 'grown-up conversations' about public sector strikes. His use of the term 'grown-up' can be interpreted as his view of trade union leaders and their members as being childish and petulant. This message is then transmitted to the population at large and many people then think of trade unions as behaving like spoilt children who unreasonably always want their own way.

In some ways, the criticisms of critical theory are similar to those of systems theory (Chapter 7). Like systems theory, critical theory seeks to address major structural issues, so critical practice is always going to be challenging. In particular, the concept of discourses and the complex and abstract ways discourses operate within society can be difficult to grasp and warrant clear explanation. Goodman (1992) is critical of the dense language used by writers within the area of critical theory, which makes it inaccessible to many people, especially those who are oppressed or on the margins of society. Tyson (2014) also argues that it is full of academic jargon. All of this has led to a further criticism of critical theory as being elitist (Gibson, 1986).

However, critical theory's description of power in everyday relationships has generally been much more accessible to social workers than those of radical social work. The need to challenge underlying assumptions in dominant discourses while examining everything closely with a critical eye became evident. In the light of this, reflective practice became critically reflective practice (Chapter 12). Language itself is powerful, and changing words and terminology can change the way people are seen; for example, patients and clients became service users, although not everyone agrees with this term either. In general terms, passive acceptance often means continued oppression. But power can be achieved through collective action and there can be greater strength in numbers.

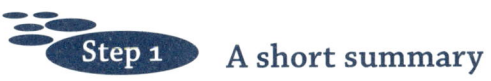 **A short summary**

Now write a short summary of critical practice by listing five key points:

1

2

3

4

5

Summarize why you feel it might be important for you as a social worker to have an understanding of critical practice.

 **Step 2** Applying critical practice to yourself

Who do you see as the ruling and powerful social groups that have influenced your life experiences so far? Make a list of them here.

Which dominant discourses can you identify that have an influence on your life?

In what ways do they operate (e.g. through the media) that confirm that you are seen without being seen? Give some examples.

How could you challenge these dominant discourses with others? Give some examples here.

Step 3   A case study from social work practice to illustrate critical practice

The Oxtown estate is a housing scheme close to the centre of a large town. Since the 1980s, the scheme has had a reputation for high rates of crime, anti-social behaviour and problems with drugs. In the last ten years, the rate of unemployment in the town has increased, and many people on the estate who have managed to find work are employed in unstable, zero-hours jobs. The local foodbank has seen a 75 per cent rise in demand and referrals to the town's Children's Services department have steadily increased, in line with national trends. You have noticed that many referrals made in respect of children now include concerns about children witnessing domestic violence at home. People on the estate tell you that they have experienced a much more punitive approach to the administration of welfare benefits in recent decades, with one young mother explaining that her family's payments were stopped for four weeks after she missed a Jobcentre appointment when she had to take her son to hospital due to a broken arm. Although there is a housing shortage, you notice that many properties on the estate have long been unoccupied and are boarded up. Many of the people who you support on the estate report issues with damp and overcrowding.

The Oxtown estate is notorious in the wider area and middle-class families avoid sending their children to the schools on the estate, preferring to commute to the outskirts of town, where the schools have received more favourable Ofsted ratings. Oxtown is regularly featured in the local press, and people from the estate find themselves being referred to as 'chavs' or 'scroungers' within the local community and on social media. There are a high number of Eastern European families living on the estate, with parents and children alike regularly experiencing racist abuse within the wider community. There is a charity shop, a budget supermarket, a takeaway and a laundrette; however, the library and Children's Centre have recently closed down.

 **Step 4**   How some knowledge of critical practice can help you to understand more about social work in Oxtown

Who are the ruling and powerful social groups in Oxtown?

Oxtown is a housing scheme which is probably run by either a housing association or a local authority. As such, these large organizations represent powerful social groups that exert a great deal of influence on the lives of the people who live there. They hold the 'purse strings' which control the amount and type of help and support that people in Oxtown receive, and they are also influenced by local and national political policies. This is demonstrated by the recent closure of the library and the Children's Centre. In addition, properties are left empty even when there is a housing shortage, and many are in a poor state of repair probably because of a lack of spending on regular maintenance.

Other powerful bodies also have significant influence on the lives of the people of Oxtown. Examples of these are the police (because of the high rates of reported crime) and central government – through the local Job Centre, which can exert its power on individuals and families by stopping benefits. The schools on the estate probably also exert strong influences through the contacts they are likely to have with social services and the probation service, in relation to safeguarding policies for their pupils and students. These organizations have the power to take children into care and to incarcerate people who 'step out of line'.

What are the dominant discourses in relation to Oxtown?

There are several dominant discourses that are evident in relation to Oxtown, giving people negative messages about life on the estate and the residents there, many of which could be unfair. The estate has a reputation locally for high rates of crime, anti-social behaviour and for problems with drugs. This projects messages of Oxtown to the wider population as an unsafe and even violent place. Because of the way discourses operate, the overall state of disrepair on the estate gives strong messages that people in Oxtown don't care about their homes and don't want to look after them. The reporting of issues of domestic violence implies that the people of Oxtown are unsafe even in their own homes.

The Ofsted ratings of the schools in the area speak of low levels of academic achievement and probably poor behaviour, and this again could give the unfair impression that parents in Oxtown don't care enough about their children to support them in their education and that they can't control them. This stops middle-class families from sending their children there, probably because they are worried about the bad influence that all of this will have on the overall development of their children.

Racist discourses give strong messages that residents from Eastern Europe shouldn't be living in Oxtown. People probably imagine that these residents are claiming all sorts of benefits, even though they might be working. Indeed, they may well be claiming benefits if they are in low-paid work, but either way, they are seen as a drain on the economy. Their children might be speakers of other languages, and the support they need in this respect might be seen as an unnecessary use of valuable and limited school resources.

Although theoretical arguments about discourses focus on language, there are visual signs in Oxtown that also give negative messages about the area and its residents. The supermarket is described as being budget, implying that the residents are poor, and have little money to spend on food. The takeaway implies that the residents eat a lot of junk food; a restaurant or even a local café serving healthy hot food would give a very different message. The only other shop is a run by a charity, which again probably implies that the residents are poor, when in fact they could be interested in recycling and helping others in the community. There is a laundrette which shows that people don't have enough money to have a washing machine or tumble dryer of their own and could also imply some kind of lack of cleanliness and personal hygiene because of the need to use these communal facilities.

We can see other strong evidence of dominant discourses in the case of Oxtown. The estate is regularly featured in the local press, and the language used is negative. You could be left wondering if anything positive is ever said about the area, even though there is good work happening there, as shown by the example of the local food bank. Social media adds to this, with references to the residents as 'chavs' or 'scroungers'. People in the wider community use these terms too.

How can these discourses be challenged?

Challenging these discourses can be best done through collective action, and as a social worker with some contacts in the community, you should be well-placed to bring groups together to work towards this end. This inevitably means that more will be achieved than through any individuals in isolation, including yourself. The local food bank could be a key partner in helping to bring this about as they will also have contacts in Oxtown and outside. As well as having links with other organizations, they will have regular and ongoing contact with significant numbers of residents. There is no mention of any kind of residents' association, and the establishment of one with the help of the food bank could be invaluable in helping the residents come together to make their voices heard. People who hold key positions of power (for example, representatives of the housing association, local authority, police force, head teachers) could be invited and would be much more likely to attend a meeting rather than appointments to speak to lots of residents individually. Also, points can be put across more strongly by groups of people than by individuals.

Step 5 — Applying critical practice to your experiences in the workplace

Think about an experience you have had in the workplace where critical practice could provide some helpful explanations. Here are some questions you could ask, with space for your responses below.

Who do you see as the ruling and powerful social groups that are influencing the lives and experiences of the local people you are in contact with in the workplace? Make a list of them here.

What are the dominant discourses that you can identify that have an influence on their lives?

In what ways do these discourses operate (e.g. through the media) that show that the individuals you encounter in your practice are seen without being seen? Give some examples.

How could you work with people accessing services to challenge the dominant discourses? Give some examples here.

CHAPTER 9

Feminism

A summary

Feminism is an important concept in social work, not least because the majority of social workers and the people they support are female. It is therefore important to understand the oppression and discrimination that women and girls face in society, in order to be ready to challenge them and seek to improve their lives. At the time of writing, women and girls make up 51 per cent of the UK's population, and as such, it is important that everyone appreciates how just over half of the population is seen. This, again, underlines the importance of understanding feminism in social work, in other professions, and indeed in life generally too.

Feminist theory is a major branch within sociology, where the focus is shifted away from a traditional male viewpoint towards that of women. This enables feminist theory to shine a light on social problems, trends and issues that are otherwise overlooked or misidentified by the historically dominant male perspective within social theory. Feminist theory helps women (and men) to understand that the way in which women perceive themselves and experience their lives is always defined and determined by men. Many of us will know the famous song by James Brown, 'It's a Man's Man's Man's World' and if any of us are unsure about this assertion, reading *Invisible Women* by Criado Perez (2020) should leave us in no doubt at all! The world as we see and experience it is based on men's assumptions.

Oppression by men is defined as patriarchy. Like critical practice, feminism recognizes the way that language communicates how women should behave – what they should and should not do. The language of patriarchy often focuses on issues of care, including care of children, elderly parents, spouses, partners and the home. Care is thought of as being in the DNA of women; something they were born to do. This often serves to trap them in low-paid and unpaid work. In my own experience, having qualified professionally and worked as a careers adviser, the advice I received from family and friends after we had our first child about my possible return to work was stark. It was also readily given by other people (especially women), even when it wasn't requested. Comments ranged from 'Obviously, it's your decision and I'll support you whatever you do but going back to work isn't something I would do in your position' to 'I wouldn't let a stranger look after my baby!' It was my mother who said to me one day, 'Please don't tell me you're thinking of giving up work! All those qualifications!' She had lived through two world wars and witnessed the hard battles women had fought to gain the vote. Suffice it to say, it was her words that I cherished when, at the end of my maternity leave, I went back to the profession I loved and had worked so hard to enter.

Feminism highlights the role of patriarchy in society, but it is also important to understand that discrimination against women is not just the work of men, because women do this too, as my own example shows. Some years ago, I attended a conference on the whole area of women in leadership in higher education. I vividly remember a keynote speech from a female vice-chancellor of a university in the UK who stated that in her experience, 'Not all sisters are sisters', as she reflected on the oppression she felt she had faced from some of her female colleagues. We shouldn't be surprised then that, at the time of writing, only 20 per cent of vice-chancellors are women, when 42 per cent of academic staff are female.

Feminist theory is focused on the following five key areas (as shown in Figure 9.1):

1. Discrimination and exclusion on the grounds of sex and gender
2. The objectification of women and girls
3. Structural and economic inequality
4. Power and oppression
5. Gender roles and stereotypes.

Feminist theory can be seen as far back as 1794 in the work of Mary Wollstonecraft. Drawing on the work of McLaughlin (2003), Milliken (2017), Foster (2018) and Wendt (2019), Payne (2021) describes the following four waves of feminist theory, and these can be closely linked with other theoretical approaches to equality. These waves can be applied not only to issues of gender but also to others, including ethnicity, disability, age and sexual orientation.

1. First wave (up to the 1930s) – focused on the political and legal rights of women to vote and own property.
2. Second wave (1960s onwards) – focused on the inequality of opportunities for women in work and public life. During this period, the term 'equal opportunities' was used, which argued that women should have the same opportunities as men in relation to such things such as work, promotion and study. This could be achieved by having a 'level playing field' where people

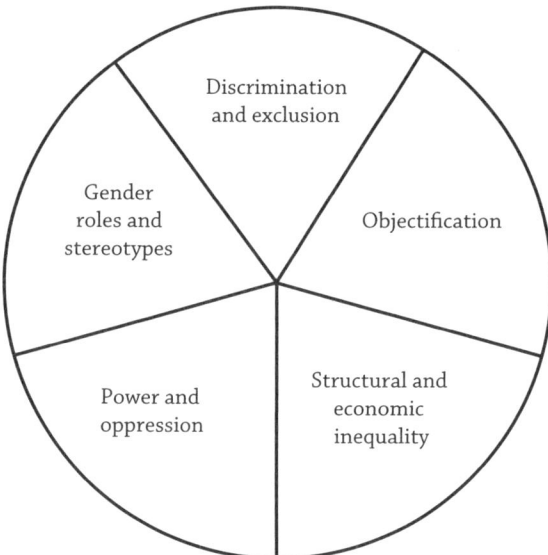

Figure 9.1 Aspects of feminism

succeed on their own merits (via a meritocracy); this can be described as a liberal approach. This period also saw the beginnings of equality legislation when the Sex Discrimination Act (SDA) came into force in 1975. This gave a strong public acknowledgement of the existence of sex discrimination in society. As a general rule, legislation is reactive. For example, before there were cars on the road, there was no need for traffic law. The SDA came about because of the acknowledgment that discrimination existed and still does. The liberal approach was challenged during this period by radicals who argued that more needed to be done because of the history of discrimination. A 'level playing field' wasn't enough and the discrimination experienced by women needed to be taken into account in order to push women's lived experiences of equality forward (Jewson and Mason, 1986).

3 Third wave (1990s onwards) – saw the advent of postmodern feminism which focused on diversity and inclusion. This valued the complexities and differences in the experiences of women and highlighted the ways in which social structures use power to subordinate women through the use of language, politics and the media. The concept of intersectionality came to the fore, showing how women can experience multiple discriminations (for example, a woman who is disabled). This third wave is also characterized by the concept of post-feminism, which argued that the objectives of feminism had been achieved.

4   Fourth wave (2010s onwards) – this focuses on the ways in which women's issues are represented through the internet and in social media. In particular, having the right to control what happens to their bodies, as well as challenging misogyny, oppression, sexism and violence against women which are common themes. A current issue at the time of writing is bringing to the fore the experiences of menopausal women and the challenges they face, particularly in the workplace.

Feminism in general seeks to challenge the discrimination that women face in the ways they are viewed by society and their lived experiences. Radical approaches mean this discrimination must be challenged. Feminism highlights the different ways that women are discriminated against, and in social work, it raises concerns for women's conditions. Women-centred practice has developed as a result, with its focus on identifying women's particular needs and seeking to respond to them. Violence in personal relationships has been a central issue along with a number of areas related to raising children. In addition, the need to reconstruct private domestic relationships on a more equal footing is identified as being important in helping women to achieve equality.

Feminism has been criticized on a number of different grounds, not least because it is seen as presenting a woman-centred viewpoint. Others argue that there is no evident leader of the feminist movement and that feminists do not agree on everything. Disagreements about some key aspects within feminism mean that it can be difficult to identify a feminist viewpoint on certain issues (Redferne and Aune, 2013). Feminism has also been criticized for being somewhat white and privileged in its approach and for failing to recognize the experiences of those women who are also marginalized through issues of poverty (Davis, 2019). Indeed, social work has faced these criticisms too (Zuffery, 2016).

Like critical practice, feminist social work argues that successful challenges and solutions to the issues that women face are best found through collective activity. Coming together with like-minded people who have had (or are having) similar experiences in life can be powerful for many people. Bringing women together to share these experiences gives women encouragement and support. As well as giving them a louder voice, it also gives them access to networks for practical help that may otherwise be unavailable.

 **A short summary**

Now write a short summary of feminism by listing five key points:

1

2

3

4

5

Summarize why you feel it might be important for you as a social worker to have an understanding of feminism.

Step 2 — Applying feminism to yourself

What does the term feminism mean to you?

From your own lived experience, highlight some key examples that demonstrate how a traditional male viewpoint regarding how women are meant to behave has influenced your thinking and behaviour.

Write some notes on times when you (or women you know well) feel you (or they) have been discriminated against on the grounds of gender.

List some of the current issues that you (or women you know well) face that demonstrate the continuing importance of feminism.

 **Step 3**   # A case study from social work practice to illustrate feminism

Abdul and Ahmed are 7-year-old twins who were recently left alone overnight whilst both parents went to work. Shazia is a support worker in a hospital and Nazir works night shifts in a factory. A neighbour alerted the police when one of the children was seen trying to open a first-floor bedroom window at 11.30 pm. The children were removed under police powers of protection and placed with foster carers for 48 days whilst safety planning could be undertaken by Children's Services. The police reported that there was no food in the fridge or cupboards and the children did not have any bedding. The children appeared dirty and were both wearing clothing which was too small for them. The home was very cold. Shazia and Nazir were both arrested and interviewed. Shazia's sister, Syeda, agreed to care for the children whilst investigations take place. Shazia and Nazir were very keen for Syeda to care for the boys, and this was arranged after preliminary checks and a home visit.

A child protection conference is arranged for two weeks' time, to consider whether the children are at risk of significant harm, and if they require a multi-agency plan to protect them. As the social worker, you liaise with other professionals as part of your assessment. The children's class teacher expresses that she is shocked that Shazia could leave her children alone overnight. She states, 'As a mother, you should always protect your children. Abdul has some learning needs too, and he would have been very scared. I knew Nazir works night shifts. Shazia will need to give up her job now, I suppose.' The GP said there are no health needs identified for the children, reporting, 'Nazir is the parent who brings the children for any medical appointments, which is very unusual. It's mothers I see in clinic with children, not fathers.' The Family Support Worker runs a parents' support group in school and said that Shazia has attended 'once or twice'. She states, 'We look at parenting techniques and strategies, which is helpful for Shazia, as Abdul can be a handful'. When you ask about Nazir's engagement, the Family Support Worker says, 'I've never met him. We've not actually invited him to group to be honest'.

Step 4 — How some knowledge of feminism can help you to understand more about Shazia and Nazir's situation

How has poverty affected this family?

It seems clear that the family concerned are living in poverty and that both parents need to work to try and make ends meet. The descriptions offered of the family's circumstances show that this continues to be a huge challenge. We are not told whether the twins being left alone at night was a rare (or even a one-off) event, or a regular occurrence. It could be that one or both of the parents might have faced a last-minute change of shifts at very short notice when a childcare option was simply not available. The couple might have feared losing their jobs and felt that they had no choice but to leave the children at home on their own. But even if that is the case, it doesn't make their actions justifiable because it clearly compromised the children's safety.

How does the language of key professionals indicate their views of the role of women in society?

The children's class teacher (a woman) expresses her shock that Shazia could leave her children alone overnight. Her views on the role of women as primary carers are crystal clear. There is absolutely no suggestion that Nazir has caring responsibilities too, but she states that it is the job of a mother to protect her children. In addition, she is clear that Shazia needs to give up her job. Shazia might earn more than Nazir, which means that on a financial level, it could make sense for Nazir to give up his job. It is impossible to ascertain this because we are simply not told.

Childcare responsibilities within the family do appear to be shared between Shazia and Nazir. Nazir takes the children to medical appointments and the GP concerned expresses their surprise at this, stating that he or she usually sees (and probably expects to see) mothers with their children, again as a way of fulfilling their primary role as carer. Likewise, the Family Support Worker admits that Nazir has never been invited to attend the parents' support group, and it seems likely that other fathers haven't been invited either, although we are not told this specifically.

What other equality issues could be at play?

Bearing in mind the likely ethnicity of the family concerned, the issues previously highlighted could also be evidence of intersectionality. Whether the responses of the key professionals concerned would have been any different if the family had been White British, we simply don't know. Assumptions about stereotypical family roles, in particular in ethnic communities, may or may not have been at work in this case. In addition, does Nazir attend the doctor's appointments because his command of the English language is better than Shazia's? Or is it simply because working night shifts means that he is more available than her? Again, we don't know.

How might this family be best supported?

Feminism argues that the best way of supporting the family is through collective action, and it seems that some key support mechanisms are in place and could be used to greater effect. Some family support through Shazia's sister Syeda is available and she is clearly willing to help. There might be other relatives who could help too. The parents' support group could be key in helping the family to identify more practical help, bringing them together with families in similar situations, and the Family Support Worker and the GP may also know of other support groups in the area. As a social worker, you might be able to introduce the family to charities and local community groups who could support them too.

Step 5 — Applying feminism to your experiences in the workplace

Think about an experience you have had in the workplace where feminism could provide some helpful explanations. Here are some questions you could ask, with space for your responses below.

From your experiences in the workplace, highlight some key examples that demonstrate a traditional male viewpoint regarding how women are meant to behave.

Write some notes on times when you have seen women being discriminated against on the grounds of gender.

List some of the current issues that you have seen in the workplace that demonstrate the continuing importance of feminism.

Describe some examples you have seen of challenging these issues collectively.

CHAPTER 10

Anti-oppressive practice

A summary

This chapter completes our review of theories that give a central position to society as distinct from those that focus on the individual. It is clear that looking at an individual's position alone is not enough when trying to understand someone's difficulties and issues, and their social context is important too. Critical theory emphasizes the ways in which dominant discourses shape social relationships, which are controlled by groups that hold power in society (see Chapter 8). Those with power seek to coerce and control those without it, which leads to oppression. Feminist theory focuses on the oppression of women and the discrimination they face (see Chapter 9). In general terms, critical and feminist theory did a lot to raise awareness of inequalities in society and of the ways in which these are perpetuated. This was at a time when other factors, in particular, issues of race, culture and ethnicity, were also coming to the fore.

You will find two terms associated with equality issues being used in literature – anti-oppressive practice and anti-discriminatory practice – and these are often used interchangeably, which can be confusing. Here, the following distinction between them is made. Discrimination is generally seen as treating someone unfairly and unjustifiably on the grounds of a particular characteristic, for example, ethnicity or gender. The focus of anti-discriminatory practice, therefore, is on challenging discrimination. Oppression is a broader term than discrimination and is a social act which places unfair and unjustifiable restrictions on people's lives. Overall, oppression serves to keep marginalized people on the margins of society. Social justice lies at the heart of all anti-oppressive practice, which seeks to increase equality and fairness through shared support and action (Howe, 2009). Its focus is on the process of oppression and exclusion rather than solely on discrimination itself.

Being culturally aware is at the heart of anti-oppressive practice, and at the centre of this is the concept of multiculturalism. Initially, multiculturalism focused on issues of ethnicity and arose from widespread concern about racism and ethnic conflict. The central argument was that the culture of people from different countries and backgrounds should be valued. This would lead to a position where different experiences would be recognized and respected, leading to an overall acceptance of diversity in society. This meant that different cultures would be seen positively, giving scope for people to learn from one another about a range of different practices as they lived side by side. Culture is now seen as a much broader term and multiculturalism is seen as part of a wider movement concerned with the experiences of all marginalized people, including, for example, those with disabilities and LGBTQ people. Again, the overall emphasis is on valuing difference and recognizing diversity.

Anti-oppressive practice means understanding that issues of power are always present in social relationships. Professional practitioners in a range of public services have power over people's lives, and it is important that this is not abused in any way. Whether it is the power of a head teacher to exclude a student from school, a police officer to arrest someone, or a social worker to remove a child from their parents or to take away someone's liberty because of mental illness, it is clear that all of this must be done with forethought, care and in a spirit of fairness.

Thompson's (2021) PCS model focuses on anti-discriminatory practice and offers a clear and useful explanation of how inequalities and discrimination are played out and perpetuated in society. His model can be used as an analytical tool and contains the following three levels:

Personal or psychological – this operates at the individual level and represents our thoughts and feelings and the behaviours that stem from them. Our personal attitudes and values also operate at this level and can include prejudices that we might hold about certain people and situations. To some extent, this level is shaped by our previous personal life experiences.

Cultural – culture operates through life experiences that are shared by people. This includes understandings and meanings, as well as the way things are done (and not done) in particular contexts. This results in patterns of behaviour that are deemed to be acceptable or unacceptable within a particular social setting. At this level, a wide range of assumptions are made, and things are taken for granted, often without any real questioning.

Structural – this operates at the social or societal level and concerns the ways in which society is organized and divided. As such, it is closely linked with issues of power. People with power usually like to keep it and want to stop others from gaining it. They control the discourses that make this happen, which constitutes oppression.

Thompson argues that the three levels of the PCS are interlinked, and that each level serves to reinforce the others, as shown in Figure 10.1. For example, an individual's attitudes influence their shared life experiences, which in turn affect how they view and interact with society's structures. Society's structures through their discourses speak of how people are viewed, which affects how individuals think and feel about others.

Anti-oppressive practice demands a structural analysis of power, in order to understand more about who has it and who doesn't and the reasons behind this. Empowerment is a key concept where practitioners work with people as partners in helping them to understand more about the influences on their lives as they enable them to assess their current situation. The relationship the practitioner has with an individual is characterized by trust and transparency as they work together to make sense of the situation. As a result, the person begins to see what they could do to improve their lives. This helps them to feel stronger, less helpless and more empowered to take some appropriate action. Howe (2009: 148) argues that, 'Power means you can determine the content of your own experience. You have the ability to control the environment to suit your needs ... have a say in plans and decisions that affect you ... a right to be heard.'

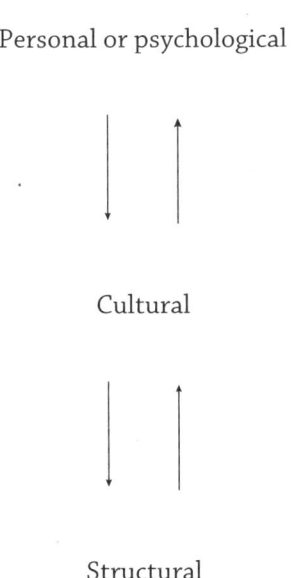

Figure 10.1 Thompson's (2021) PCS analysis

Critics of anti-oppressive practice can be somewhat difficult to find because who would openly argue against it as a general principle? However, Cocker and Hafford-Letchfield (2014) argue that anti-discriminatory practice and anti-oppressive practice have lost their political edge and have become part of status quo thinking. In addition, Dominelli (2002) critiques Thompson's PCS model for its somewhat narrow focus on discrimination and argues for a broader emphasis on oppression. The term 'empowerment' also has its critics and McLaughlin (2016: 53) argues that in spite of it being 'held to be a self-evident good', it lacks clear definition as a term. Without this, people can interpret it 'in any way they choose' (McLaughlin, 2016: 56). McLaughlin cites examples of situations when the term 'empowerment' only serves to keep people in a place of submission. One example is psychiatric patients who are asked to contribute to their healthcare plan whilst not being allowed to refuse prescribed medication. However, as the case study in this chapter shows, for people living in the community, the choice of whether to take their prescribed medication remains theirs. In addition, it is somewhat ironic that the term 'empowerment' has often been linked with the self-help movement, which is highly individualistic in nature.

In spite of this, like other approaches that place society at the centre rather than the individual, anti-oppressive practice is often implemented most effectively via groups and communities (Howe, 2009) as people meet together to discuss ways of improving their circumstances through joint action. It is often easier to achieve change when working together with others than for individuals to do so on their own. Self-help groups of like-minded people can be particularly effective in enabling and empowering people to bring about change in their own lives and in the lives of those in the community who share similar experiences.

Step 1 — A short summary

Now write a short summary of anti-oppressive practice by listing five key points:

1

2

3

4

5

Summarize why you feel it might be important for you as a social worker to have an understanding of anti-oppressive practice.

 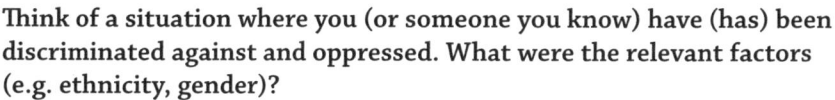

Step 2 — Applying anti-oppressive practice to yourself

Think of a situation where you (or someone you know) have (has) been discriminated against and oppressed. What were the relevant factors (e.g. ethnicity, gender)?

Thinking about your own levels of self-awareness, how culturally aware would you say you are, and why?

How do you feel you need to grow and develop in this particular area and how might you do this?

Using the headings of Thompson's PCS model, describe some of the insights you have gained into your own experiences of inequality and discrimination, and of others you know.

Personal or psychological

Cultural

Structural

Describe any self-help groups you know of or have been involved in and how they have empowered their members.

Step 3 — A case study from social work practice to illustrate anti-oppressive practice

Geoffrey (86) is a Jamaican man who has lived in the UK for the last forty years, after emigrating with his mother who died twenty years ago. Throughout his adult life, Geoffrey has experienced periods of severe mental illness and was diagnosed with schizoaffective disorder in his 40s, although he does not agree with this diagnosis and chooses not to take medication. Geoffrey hears voices, which he describes as 'friendly', and is well-known within his local community, attending a lunchtime club at the community centre every week. Over the years, Geoffrey has been periodically admitted to hospital under the Mental Health Act (1983) when experiencing periods of intense distress but typically has periods of stability lasting years between admissions.

With age, Geoffrey's physical health has begun to deteriorate. He experiences palpitations and has also had several falls in public over the last six months which have required ambulance attendance. Usually a cheerful and outgoing man, these changes have impacted upon Geoffrey's confidence and sense of self-esteem. Carers visit Geoffrey each morning to help him get dressed, keep on top of the cleaning and prepare his meals for the day. He has no family support but speaks to his ex-partner Rose, who lives in Jamaica, by telephone once per week.

Recently, Geoffrey has become the target of harassment from a local group of young people. The teenagers have been seen congregating outside Geoffrey's home and on one occasion were spoken to by the police. You receive an urgent phone call to say that Geoffrey has been arrested outside a charity shop in the town centre after an altercation with a group of young men. One of the teenagers has suffered a broken nose and CCTV footage confirms that Geoffrey has hit the young person in the face. Geoffrey is in an agitated state and is being held in a police cell. The parents of the young person involved are furious and have contacted the local press, stating that people like Geoffrey should not be allowed out in the community unsupervised.

Step 4 — How some knowledge of anti-oppressive practice can help you to understand more about Geoffrey's case

How and why might Geoffrey experience discrimination?

As a Jamaican man, Geoffrey is likely to have experienced some discrimination in his life on the grounds of his ethnicity, although we are not told this explicitly. As an older man who has suffered from severe mental illness, it is fair to say that issues of intersectionality apply to Geoffrey and that he will have been subject to a range of disadvantages because of his age and his mental health issues, as well as his ethnicity. Geoffrey's case also demonstrates the application of multicultural approaches because he is clearly suffering from multiple disadvantages that are having a big impact on his life.

How might Geoffrey feel as a result of this?

Geoffrey is currently experiencing harassment from young people in his community who have been targeting him, as shown by the recent incident where a group congregated outside his home. This is likely to have made him feel very anxious and even frightened, especially as he lives alone. He is also becoming weaker physically, which is evidenced by a number of falls he has had in recent months; this all adds to his growing lack of confidence and self-esteem. His recent arrest is likely to be an indication of the high levels of stress caused by the intimidation from the group of young men.

How can Thompson's PCS model be applied to Geoffrey's case?

Personal or psychological – we don't know a lot about Geoffrey's position at this level, but we do know that he doesn't accept his diagnosis of schizoaffective disorder and chooses not to take medication. This suggests that his views of his own mental illness are different from those of the professionals seeking to support him, and perhaps of others around him too. In relation to the young people concerned, they seem to view Geoffrey as a target. This could be because of his ethnicity, age and mental health, but again we are not told this specifically.

Cultural – it is clear that assumptions are being made about Geoffrey and his situation. This is shown by the parents of the young man that Geoffrey hit, who have contacted the local press. The phrase 'people like Geoffrey' is powerful derogatory language and the parents articulate their views clearly when they state that people like him 'should not be allowed out in the community unsupervised'. This gives strong messages to people in the local community who are likely to assume that Geoffrey is some kind of threat and someone who can't control his anger. This is likely to prompt fear in those who read about this incident and means that Geoffrey becomes someone to avoid and watch, rather than someone who is usually cheerful and mild mannered and who needs support.

Structural – Geoffrey has had direct dealings with people from powerful groups in society. These probably include social workers who would have been involved in admitting him to hospital under the Mental Health Act (1983) and the police regarding his current arrest. The local press can also be seen to operate at this level as they perpetuate discourses about people with mental health issues through Geoffrey's story.

What does working with Geoffrey in an anti-oppressive way involve?

This is best done through helping him to access appropriate local groups and enabling them to support him. This all needs to be done in a relationship of trust and transparency so that he feels empowered. Geoffrey already attends a lunch club at a local community centre every week, which is likely to be a good source of support for him, and there could be other groups in the community that could provide more. These might include groups run by charities that support people with mental illness, although it is very possible that Geoffrey himself will not see these as being appropriate for him. Other groups supporting older people in the community might be more amenable to Geoffrey though, and the support he could gain here might help him to feel more able to cope with his current situation. Discussions in the groups could include strategies for coping with his high levels of stress, and hopefully he would also gain some moral support from people in similar situations, which could help him feel less alone. In his current position and in the future, he might need help from victim support either individually or in a group.

As a social worker, there is also a role for influential work that can be done with young people in the area by some important key players. This might involve linking up with schools, colleges and other organizations that work with young people in the area to help to inform their work in relation to formal and informal education on the subject of challenging discrimination in relation to ethnicity, age and mental illness. These will already be important areas of the curriculum and speaking with them about the generalities of a case like Geoffrey's could help them to bring this vital educational work to life.

Step 5 — Applying anti-oppressive practice to your experiences in the workplace

Think about an experience you have had in the workplace where anti-oppressive practice could provide some helpful explanations. Here are some questions you could ask, with space for your responses below.

Think of a situation that you have encountered in the workplace where an individual has been discriminated against and oppressed. What were the relevant factors (e.g. ethnicity, gender)?

Thinking about your own levels of self-awareness, how has this experience helped you to gain more cultural awareness?

How might you be able to learn more in relation to this during your time in the workplace?

Using the headings of Thompson's PCS model, describe some of the insights you have gained into issues of inequality and discrimination from the workplace.

Personal or psychological

Cultural

Structural

Describe any self-help groups you have come across in the area and try to find out how they have empowered their members.

CHAPTER 11

Person-centred approaches

A summary

Having considered theoretical approaches that focus on the individual and those that put social and societal aspects at the centre, this chapter seeks to bring these two groups of theories together by considering an approach that can be described as more holistic.

Person-centred approaches have their roots in Rogerian humanistic personal counselling (Rogers, 1951), which, at the time of its publication, was somewhat revolutionary. It represented a distinct move from psychodynamics and behaviourism (where the practitioner is seen as the expert) to an emphasis on the importance of what the client sees in themselves. From this perspective, the individual is seen as the expert on the subject of their own life. In his early work, Rogers (1951) used the term 'client-centredness' to describe his approach but later began to use the term 'person-centredness' (Rogers, 1980), to indicate a wider and more holistic view of the client as a person and their relationships with others, in particular, the counsellor.

The self-concept is central to Rogers' work and can be defined as the beliefs we hold about ourselves. He argues that the self-concept is influenced by the following three factors:

1 Our parents' attitudes towards us, especially when we were very young (our early environment)
2 The beliefs we hold about ourselves (our internal world)
3 Our perceptions of others (our external world).

Central to Rogers' argument is that all individuals have a strong desire to self-actualize; in other words, to achieve their full potential. In this particular area, his work appears to have much in common with Maslow's (1943) early work on his hierarchy of needs. Rogers saw personal growth as being at the core of the counselling process, which can happen effectively given the right conditions.

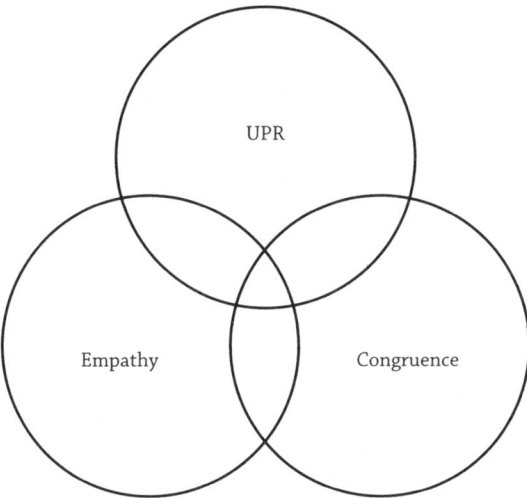

Figure 11.1 Conditions for therapeutic change

Rogers called these the core conditions for therapeutic change (shown in Figure 11.1) and are as follows:

- Empathy – the ability to understand the experiences and feelings of others. This is sometimes described as being able to walk in another person's shoes (and even in their sweaty socks as well!)
- Congruence – this means being real, authentic and genuine with clients. Congruence happens when a practitioner's inner experience and outward expression match. By being authentic, the practitioner shows they can be trusted, which is vital in building a good working relationship with the client.
- Unconditional positive regard (UPR) – put simply, this is about seeing the good in people irrespective of their life experiences and actions. It involves respecting the individual as a human being who has free will and operates under the assumption that he or she is doing the best they can in their given circumstances.

These core conditions form 'the interpersonal climate' that facilitate and encourage what Rogers called 'the actualising tendency' (Joseph, 2003: 304). This actualizing tendency is what motivates people to grow and develop, and Rogers argues that this is innate in everyone.

When the core conditions are present, a practitioner with effective counselling skills can enable the client to engage with their actualizing tendency to bring about change through critical reflection on their own lives. This is best put in Rogers' own words: 'Individuals have in themselves vast resources for self-understanding and for altering their self-concepts, basic attitudes, and self-directed behavior; these resources can be tapped if a definable climate of facilitative psychological attitudes can be provided' (Rogers, 1980: 115).

Some effective counselling skills that are appropriate for practitioners in the helping professions including social work are as follows:

- Active listening – this involves listening intently to what the client is saying and showing them that you are doing so (for example, by reflecting back using phrases such as 'If I've heard you correctly …' or 'You seem to be saying …', open body language and a good amount of eye contact)
- Summarizing – this also helps the client to feel that they have been heard and can help to keep a discussion focused. Summarizing involves reflecting back on what they have been saying in order to condense the main points of a discussion. Hearing a summary can help the client reflect and gives them the opportunity to adjust their words if they want to.
- Paraphrasing – like active listening, this can help the practitioner to check that they have heard the client correctly and again gives them the opportunity to say whether or not this is the case. For example, a phrase like 'You seem to be saying … Is that how you see things too, or might you phrase things differently?' can work well.

Person-centredness means being non-directive and puts the client 'in the driving seat'. If they are the expert on their own life, it is not for the practitioner to suggest or direct in any way, and the process works best when the client discovers the way forward themselves because they then own the process. But to achieve this, the client needs to be committed to the process and active within it, otherwise it will not be successful. Overall, the aim is for the client to achieve greater independence and to cope better with situations they face now and in the future. They must not be encouraged to develop an unhealthy dependence on the practitioner. All of this is achieved through a process of deep reflection (see Chapter 12).

In a critique of client-centredness, Masson (1988) questions whether or not the core conditions are possible with all clients; for example, can a practitioner have UPR for a client with a conviction for a serious violent offence? Rogers (1959) argues that there are times when a relationship with a client can falter or fail to develop for some reason and argues that practitioners don't and indeed can't always demonstrate UPR. Here, he describes the positive regard as 'selective', as distinct from unconditional (Rogers, 1959: 237). He also states that empathy will not always be achievable. In these situations, the practitioner suspends their judgement of the person in order to remain neutral. However, some writers such as Corey, Schneider Corey and Callanan (2007) argue that total neutrality is impossible to achieve and point to the concept of reflexivity (see Chapter 12). In relation to social work practice, Teater (2020) argues that taking a person-centred approach might not always be possible within the demands of professional practice, particularly in relation to time. She also points to times and circumstances where a social worker might need to be directive because of agency constraints.

Whilst Rogers used the term 'person-centredness' in relation to therapy, it also began to be used outside this context, including in health and social care. A person-centred approach (sometimes called a person-led approach) is where the individual is supported to lead their own care and is treated holistically. The focus is on the person and what they can do, not on their circumstances, condition or disability. Support should focus on achieving the person's aspirations and be tailored to their needs and unique circumstances. A person-centred approach also means focusing on the individual's context and on the elements of care, support and treatment that matter most, not only to them but also to their family and carers. The priority here is to identify what is most important to everyone concerned, without making assumptions. This is also one of the key elements of reflexivity (see Chapter 12).

Step 1 — A short summary

Now write a short summary of person-centred approaches by listing five key points:

1

2

3

4

5

Summarize why you feel it might be important for you as a social worker to have an understanding of person-centred approaches.

 **Step 2**   Applying person-centred approaches to yourself

Think about your own self-concept and summarize the influences of the three areas that Rogers identifies.

1. My parents' or carers' attitudes

2. My beliefs about myself

3. My perceptions of others around me

How would you assess yourself in relation to the core conditions?
- Empathy

- Congruence

- UPR

How would you describe your actualizing tendency?

How would you assess your key interpersonal skills? Give an example of each.
- Active listening

- Summarizing

- Paraphrasing

 **Step 3** # A case study from social work practice to illustrate person-centred approaches

Steven (53) is a man with a significant learning disability who has always been cared for by his parents. Steven communicates non-verbally, using a few Makaton signs including 'mum', 'biscuit', 'car' and 'bathroom'. He loves listening to music from the 1970s and is interested in cars. Steven is described by carers as being 'a pleasant man who can occasionally display challenging behaviour'. Steven's father John died eighteen months ago following a short illness, and his mother Helen (84) has been caring for Steven independently since this time. Steven has a sister, Jean (48), who visits once per week and helps Helen to manage the family finances. Jean is a single parent to three teenage children and works full-time in retail.

You receive an urgent referral in respect of Steven after Helen has been admitted to hospital following a fall. Helen has sustained a fracture to her hip and will need to spend around six weeks in hospital and a rehabilitation facility before she is fit to return home. Hospital staff are concerned that Helen was underweight when she was found to have fallen and has several large bruises on her body which she says have happened when she has been trying to help Steven get changed.

You arrange an emergency placement for Steven in a residential home for people with learning disabilities, where he takes some time to settle in, making the Makaton sign for 'mum' and appearing unhappy whenever his sister Jean goes to visit. Care staff report that Steven seems to enjoy interacting with other residents and going out in the car with staff but can become aggressive when being supported with his personal care. Helen is very distressed by the thought of Steven being in a residential home and feels that she has let her husband down by 'allowing' this to happen. Helen is adamant that Steven will be returning to live with her when she has recovered from her injury, while Jean feels worried about Helen's ability to cope.

Step 4 — How some knowledge of person-centred approaches can help you to understand more about Steven's case

What would working with Steven in a person-centred way involve?

This means focusing on Steven and what he can do, not on his circumstances or his disability. Steven is described as having a severe learning disability, but even so, there are things that he can do and that he enjoys. These form an important part of Steven's life and give him continuity, satisfaction and pleasure. He is clearly close to his mum, and we know that he is missing her while he is in the residential home because he seems to be asking for her. From a person-centred perspective, Steven should be viewed holistically which means taking into account the mental and social factors that affect him and not just the symptoms of the condition he presents. Steven needs to be viewed as a whole person in his circumstances and in the context of his family.

There are some important people in Steven's life and working in a person-centred way also means focusing on the elements of care and support that matter most, not only to Steven but also to his mum and his sister Jean. In addition, we are told that Steven enjoys communicating with other residents in the care home and hopefully he has started to make friends there. He also has carers at home who hopefully have been building a good relationship with him for some time since the death of his father.

What evidence is there for Steven's self-concept and actualizing tendency and for those of close family members?

Steven certainly has a self-concept, but it is difficult to know very much about it because of the communication difficulties he has. His actualizing tendencies are also unclear but probably link with those things he enjoys and gains satisfaction from. He seems to have a close and loving relationship with his mum who has no doubt offered him a lot of safety and security over the years. The same can probably be said of his Dad, who died eighteen months ago. Steven's mum believes that she should be looking after Steven and sees this as her role, especially since the death of Steven's dad. She feels guilty about not being able to do this at the moment and may well feel the same about it in relation to the future. Her actualizing tendency is probably linked with the care she wants to give to Steven.

Steven's sister, Jean, clearly has a lot of family responsibilities herself and is worried about the impact that looking after Steven is having on her mum, especially now that she is on her own and, of course, getting older. Her actualizing tendency might also include her caring role for her own children as well as offering support to her mum and Steven. Steven is unhappy when he sees Jean, and it is difficult to know why this might be. Jean is clearly worried about the situation, and she might see Steven as a burden on their mum. She might also be unhappy about the way he treats her in relation to his personal care. It's possible that Steven may have picked up on some tensions between Helen and Jean, but put simply, we don't know because we aren't told. Person-centred approaches argue strongly that we shouldn't make assumptions.

What will be needed in order to work with Steven and his family members in a person-centred way and achieve their aspirations?

This will mean demonstrating the three core conditions of empathy, congruence and UPR in order to build a trusting and effective relationship. It will mean using the key interpersonal skills of active listening, summarizing and paraphrasing. It also means focusing on enabling them to achieve their aspirations and this needs to be tailored to their needs and unique circumstances. Steven lies at the centre of this process, but the position of other family members needs to be taken into account too. This is where things become complex for a number of reasons. It's difficult to know what Steven's aspirations are because of the difficulties he has with communication. This means it will be very important to listen to him and to those people who know him best, including family members and carers. Helen clearly has aspirations for Steven's care and how she sees her role within this. Jean worries about the effect of all of this on her mum especially in the longer term.

Are there any possible underlying issues?

It seems important to remember that this is a family who are all grieving the loss of Steven's dad, John. There seem to be particular issues with Steven's personal care, and we can only wonder whether or not John took responsibility for this in the past. This could mean that Steven finds this change particularly difficult to cope with and the aggression he shows in relation to this (both at home and in the residential home) is currently the only way he knows of showing his sadness. This cannot be assumed but is certainly a topic worthy of discussion with everyone concerned.

 **Step 5** — **Applying person-centred approaches to your experiences in the workplace**

Think about an experience you have had in the workplace where person-centred approaches could provide some helpful explanations. Here are some questions you could ask, with space for your responses below.

Think about the client's self-concept and summarize the influences of the three areas that Rogers identifies.

1 Their parents' or carers' attitudes

2 Their beliefs about themselves

3 Their perceptions of others around them

How would you assess yourself and other practitioners working on this case in relation to the core conditions?
- Empathy

- Congruence

- UPR

How would you describe the client's actualizing tendency and that of the other people who are involved in the case?

How would you assess your key interpersonal skills and those of other practitioners working on this case? Give an example of each.

- Active listening

- Summarizing

- Paraphrasing

CHAPTER 12

Critically reflective practice

A summary

So far in this book, we have examined theories that place the individual at the centre, followed by those that emphasize the role of society in general and the client's social context. In the previous chapter, person-centred approaches were discussed, where the client's perspectives, experiences, social relationships and circumstances are all seen to be relevant. The subject of this final chapter in Part 1 is critically reflective practice which considers a number of theories and concepts, this time applied mainly to the social worker as distinct from the client. This paves the way for Part 2, where multiple theoretical approaches are applied to three case studies and the social workers who seek to support them. The emphasis of critically reflective practice is on the self and although we concentrate mostly on the practitioner in this chapter, the concepts covered can also be applied effectively to work with the people social workers support. The word 'critically' has been applied to reflective practice in recent years, and this marks a significant development in thinking, from reflection as a process to reflexivity as a stance (Fook, 2022).

Reflective practice as an approach grew from the work of Dewey (1933) who argued that reflective thought plays an important part in helping us to learn from experience and underpins a reflective cycle. Many writers built on his work, developing their own reflective cycles, and Kolb (1984) is probably the most well-known of these. In general terms, as we reflect on an experience we have had, we analyse and evaluate the detail of it in order to build new professional knowledge as we prepare for the next experience. Fook and Gardner (2007) describe this as a process of deconstruction and reconstruction, which involves analysis and change. This ensures that our practice is continually moving forward as our knowledge grows and deepens.

Other writers have also developed learning cycles, and each has a slightly different emphasis. Examples here are Gibbs' (1988) reflective cycle and the work of Boud, Keogh and Walker (1985) who emphasize reflecting on feelings, and Mezirow (1978, 1981) and Argyris and Schön (1974) who encourage us to examine our assumptions through their seven levels of reflection and double loop learning cycles respectively. More recently, Illeris (2014) drawing on the work of Taylor (2009) focuses on reflection as part of a holistic process of transformational learning. My own work (Bassot, 2020) has sought to bring these various aspects together in my Integrated Reflective Cycle (see Figure 12.1) The cycle encourages us to take a questioning approach to professional practice and is an excellent way of delving deeper into not only what we did, but why; this is a key feature of critically reflective practice. There are four points on the cycle, which starts with an experience that we are encouraged to describe. We are then asked to reflect on it in order to interrogate our approach. This includes an examination of the feelings we experienced and any assumptions we might have been making. In the third point on the cycle, we examine how this experience can contribute to our professional knowledge. The final step on the cycle asks us to look forward in order to examine how we might use this knowledge and experience in the future, including the strategies that could be used next time to help us to be more effective.

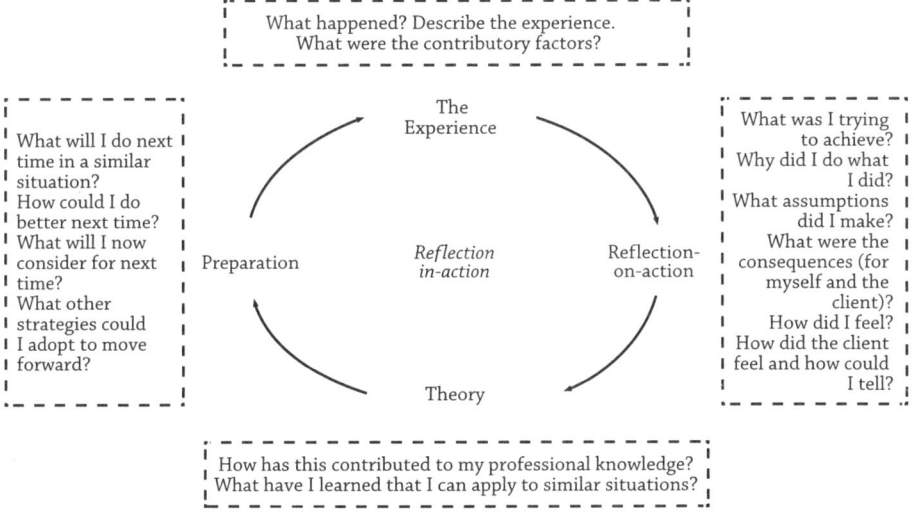

Figure 12.1 The Integrated Reflective Cycle

Any introduction to reflective practice would not be complete without a discussion of Schön's seminal book, *The Reflective Practitioner*. Here, he describes what he calls 'reflection-in-action', and this is the kind of thinking we all do as we are working, studying and living our daily lives. As human beings, we all have the capacity to think as we are doing other things and Schön (1983: 54) describes this as 'thinking on your feet'. In the book, he places less of an emphasis on what he calls 'reflection-on-action'. This is the kind of thinking professionals do after an experience, which is seen as a key element of many of the reflective cycles discussed earlier.

Critically reflective practice raises the importance of the whole area of self-awareness. As we continue to know and understand ourselves better, we become better placed to support others, who take part in a process of getting to know themselves better too. Knowing ourselves involves understanding the things that influence our thinking. These include:

- Values – these are things that are important to us, and in a very literal sense, they are things that we value. They are deep rooted, and often stem from our upbringing, thereby reflecting our social context. They can include personal qualities like honesty, dedication and the role of family.
- Emotions – these are described by Williams and Penman (2011: 19) as a combination of thoughts, feelings, impulses and bodily sensations (such as a faster heart rate or trembling hands) that create 'an overall guiding theme or state of mind'.
- Assumptions – these are things we assume to be true that Brookfield (1995: 2) describes as 'taken-for-granted beliefs about the world and our place within it that seem so obvious as not to need stating explicitly'.

These three influences form a key part of our worldview: our own individual way of seeing and understanding the world around us. Our worldview influences what we do, how and why we do things in particular ways, and plays an important part in the way we interact with others.

Reflexivity underpins critically reflective practice, which demands a high level of self-awareness. Reflexivity means being aware of how we think, feel and act including the assumptions we might be making. In addition, it makes us aware of issues of power both in relationships and in organizations. This means understanding who has power in a given situation and who does not. As professional practitioners, it is always worth bearing in mind that most people we are supporting will assume that they have less power than we do. It is also worth remembering that language is a powerful tool through which we can both challenge and reinforce inequality.

There are several ways that we can reflect critically on our practice and here are two important ones:

- Keeping a reflective diary or journal – writing by hand has many benefits and in particular it helps us to slow down in our hectic professional lives. It also helps us to process our feelings as we externalize them, delve into our assumptions and consider issues of power. All of this helps us to develop our understanding of professional practice and our commitment to equality and social justice.
- Supervision – this can be done one to one or in a group and enables us to reflect on our practice in a regular and deep way. It helps us to offload and to view our practice from a number of different perspectives. It gives us an opportunity to receive feedback and challenges our critical thinking.

Critically reflective practice has its critics, and three particular points stand out. First, is the abstract nature of critically reflective practice. Ixer (1999) argues that as a term it is difficult to define, which in turn can make it difficult to assess. Second, it seems to lack rigour, relying too heavily on reflection-in-action that takes place in the moment, leading to informal knowledge. Usher and Bryant (1989) question how much reflection-in-action actually takes place and argue that practitioners tend to 'play it safe', relying on their own methods that have worked well in the past rather than challenging their thinking. Third, personal accounts of practitioners (both written and in supervision) can be used as a form of surveillance when they are brought out into the open. This often results in accounts becoming selective and guarded, and often thereby making them less helpful for professional development. Yip (2006) argues that critical reflection needs to happen in a supportive environment to prevent it from becoming destructive. Saltiel (2010) helpfully brings together a useful critique of a number of different aspects.

However, critically reflective practice plays an important part in helping practitioners to continue to grow and develop in their professional lives, as they seek to empower the people they support and to challenge inequality. In addition, it helps them to cope with the busyness and stresses of professional practice by supporting their wellbeing and building their professional resilience.

 **Step 1** A short summary

Now write a short summary of critically reflective practice by listing five key points:

1

2

3

4

5

Summarize why you feel it might be important for you as a social worker to have an understanding of critically reflective practice.

 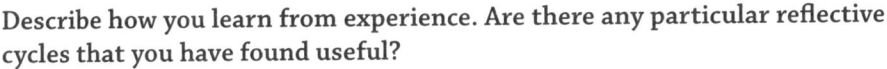

Step 2 — Applying critically reflective practice to yourself

Describe how you learn from experience. Are there any particular reflective cycles that you have found useful?

Describe your values and consider who influenced their development.

What comes to mind when you think about your emotions? Are there any situations in your professional practice where you are particularly likely to have an emotional response? If so, why do you think this is?

Describe some of the assumptions you feel you make on a regular basis. How might you begin to challenge these?

How would you describe your relationship with people you work to support in relation to power? How might you want to grow in this particular area?

Describe the reflective tools you have used. Which have been the most and least helpful and why?

 **Step 3**   # A case study from social work practice to illustrate critically reflective practice

Jude is training to be a social worker and is finding the course rewarding but challenging. Jude decided to enter the social work profession because of a deep desire to support people in difficult circumstances and wanting to make a difference. Experience in the workplace has been extremely useful and has given Jude a clear picture of what professional practice is like and the demands it makes on its practitioners. Workplaces are busy and pressurized, and Jude regularly sees practitioners who speak of their heavy workloads and high stress levels. In addition, the lives of people accessing services are very challenging too in various different respects, which is also beginning to take its toll on Jude.

Jude's current experience is with a service helping and supporting elderly people and a particular case has raised lots of concerns. Fred and Mabel are a couple in their 90s who have been together for over sixty years. They are both relatively fit and able to live independently in their retirement home. They enjoy having people around them and are happy to be involved in some of the social activities on offer. Mabel enjoys singing in the choir and Fred loves reading and regularly attends the book group. They both like going to the restaurant for lunch where they meet their friends and neighbours. Recently, Fred has become ill and seems tired and listless. He has now been diagnosed with a form of cancer that doctors are saying is inoperable and untreatable because of his age. Mabel has been hit very hard by this news and wonders how she will cope without him.

Jude accompanies a social worker on a routine visit to Fred and Mabel and meets their daughter Julia, who is angry about the lack of an offer of surgery or treatment for her father. During the discussion, Jude feels overcome by emotion and is surprised by the intensity of the feelings that this experience evokes. Jude manages to hold back tears but can feel both hands shaking and a fast heartbeat. On the way home, Jude meets up with a friend and is reminded of the experiences they both share of supporting their elderly parents and of coping with the loss of good friends and family members from cancer. Jude decides to begin to process this recent encounter with Fred and Mabel in order to learn from it and to build professional resilience.

# Step 4   How some knowledge of critically reflective practice can help you to understand more about Jude's case

Which reflective cycles might Jude use and why?

Jude could use a number of reflective cycles in order to reflect on the experience with Fred and Mabel. Some of the most appropriate might be that of Gibbs' (1988) and Boud et al., (1985) because they both emphasize the importance of reflecting on feelings. In particular, Gibbs (1988) poses questions that Jude could think about in relation to Fred and Mabel's case. For example, 'What were you thinking and feeling?' and 'What was good and bad about the experience?'

What do we know about Jude's values?

Jude decided to go into social work because of a deep desire to support people in difficult circumstances and wants to make a difference. This speaks of Jude's personal values of caring and support and suggests someone who puts the needs of others before their own. It also suggests a worldview where ideally these needs are met whenever possible. Jude undoubtedly values people and respects what they have to offer irrespective of their age and situation.

What might have prompted Jude's response to Fred and Mabel's situation?

Jude has a deeply emotional response to meeting Fred and Mabel and is no doubt reminded of current and past experiences of supporting elderly parents and of dealing with diagnoses of cancer among friends and family. Jude has also lost people to cancer and is no doubt reminded of this as well. Encountering Julia's anger might reinforce thoughts and memories that Jude has had. Jude might have experienced anger like Julia, but we don't know because we aren't told.

What assumptions might Jude be making?

Jude might be making assumptions in relation to Fred and Mabel's case, but we are not given any detail here. It could be that Jude's own parents are in a similar situation, but equally it could be that their situation is very different. They might be living happily and independently at home, or they could be struggling at home or living in a care home. Whatever circumstances Jude's parents are in, Jude has seen close family members become older, possibly raising questions in relation to their safety. This could cause a level of anxiety for Jude, and it could

Critically reflective practice   151

be that Jude wishes things were different for them in some way. In relation to Fred's diagnosis, Jude might assume like Julia that more needs to be done to protect his life at all costs.

Who holds the power in Fred and Mabel's situation?

Fred, Mabel and Julia are likely to feel powerless in this situation. Medical professionals have made a diagnosis and do not feel that surgery or treatment is an option. In a situation like this, they have difficult decisions to make and can be seen as the people with power over life and death. Julia's anger might indicate that she feels they need to do more. Equally, she is probably worried about how her mum will cope on her own.

How might Jude reflect on this experience?

Jude could use some tools to reflect on this experience. Writing in a journal could help Jude to delve deeper into the emotional side of the experience and could unearth more assumptions that were being made. Jude could make notes on the experience and take these to a supervision session. This could help Jude to unpick the experience further and to gain some different insights into it.

 **Step 5** — Applying critically reflective practice to your experiences in the workplace

Think about an experience you have had in the workplace where critically reflective practice can help you to reach some helpful explanations. Here are some questions you could ask, with space for your responses below.

Write a short description of it here.

Describe how you learned from this. Were there any particular reflective cycles that you found useful?

What impact did your values have on this case?

What was your emotional response and why do you think you reacted in this way?

What assumptions did you feel you were making and how might you begin to challenge these?

How would you describe your relationship with the people concerned in relation to power? How might you want to grow in this particular area?

Describe the reflective tools you have used to help you reflect on this case critically. Which have been the most and least helpful, and why?

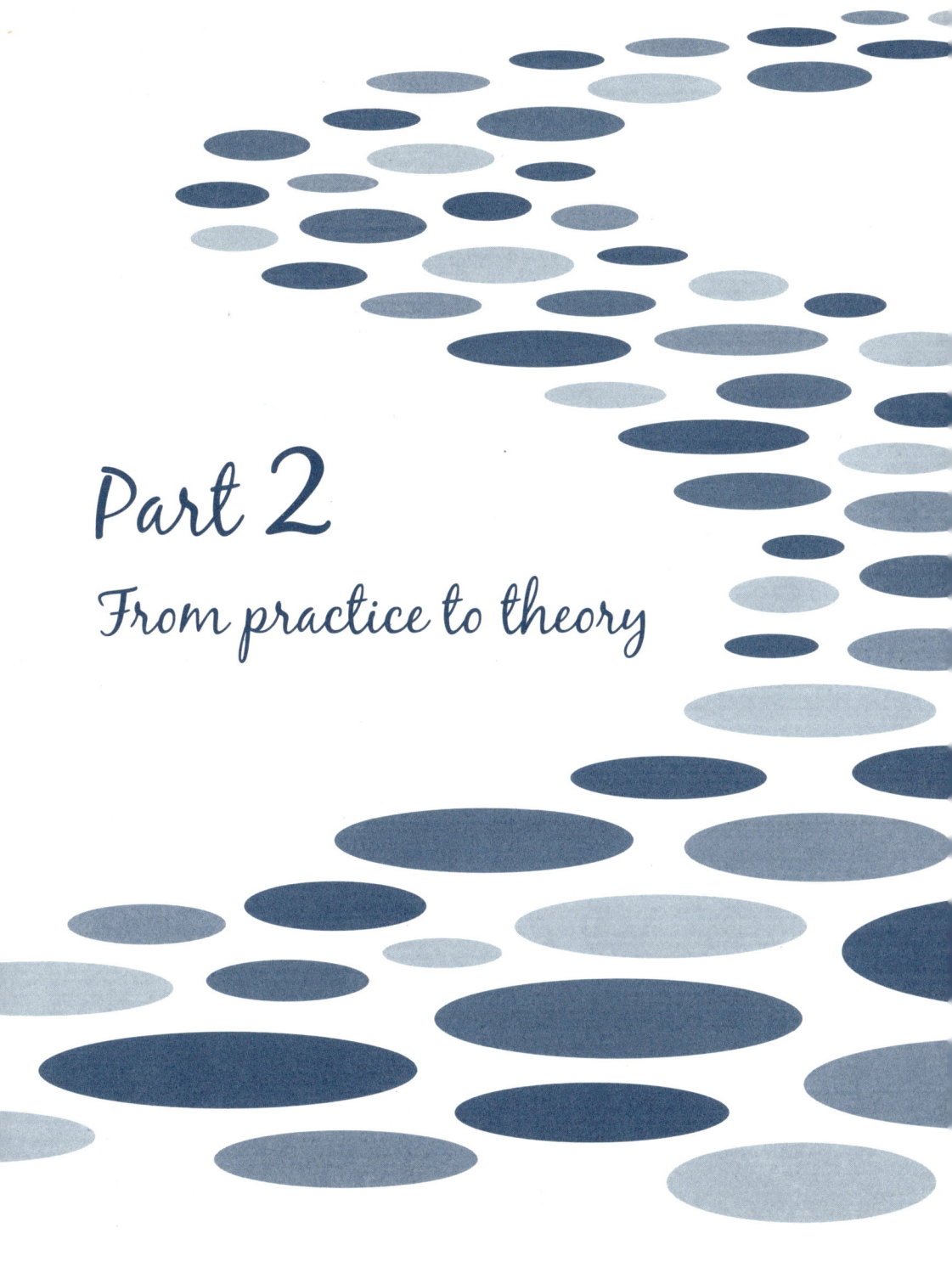
Part 2
From practice to theory

It is fair to say that no single theory can give all the insights we need into people's lives. So, in Part 2, we examine three complex case studies where a number of different theories can be applied in order to understand each of them better. Each of the theories covered in Part 1 is employed in relation to one case, and your position as a social worker is reflected on in each case study using critically reflective practice frameworks. In each case study, the following three steps are taken:

Step 1: A complex case study from social work practice is described

Step 2: Selecting which theories might apply by identifying key words and phrases and posing some questions, followed by a table showing the links made

Step 3: A discussion of how particular theories apply.

Case Study 1   Jack

Step 1

Jack is a 28-year-old, White British male who has recently been referred to your service after suffering a traumatic brain injury eighteen months ago, following a fall from some scaffolding in the town centre while intoxicated. The accident has left Jack with some mild cognitive impairments and significant physical disabilities, requiring the use of an electric wheelchair. Prior to his injury, Jack was a very active and outgoing person. He has a 3-year-old son, Jayden, who lives with Jack's ex-partner Michaela. Jack and Michaela's relationship ended when Jayden was a baby. However, until Jack's accident, they were able to co-parent amicably, and he cared for Jayden regularly at weekends. Jack's parents now take Jayden to visit his dad every month.

Jack spent a year in an inpatient rehabilitation unit after his accident and worked hard to improve his capabilities. He was motivated to be discharged so that he could live a more independent life. Jack has a lively personality and a great sense of humour. He was regularly visited by friends from work and his rugby team and joked that he was looking forward to getting back on the pitch. After leaving the unit, Jack moved into supported accommodation. A team of support workers help Jack with tasks such as washing, dressing and taking his medication during the day and a staff member sleeps over at the house every night. Jack's parents are in contact by phone every evening, speaking to the support workers about Jack's day and his progress. When they visit, they also regularly review his care file.

Jack has been referred to your service as his family and care team are becoming increasingly concerned about changes in his mood and behaviour. Jack has recently become withdrawn, referring to himself and other people with disabilities using derogatory and oppressive language and saying that he wishes he had never survived the accident. Visits from Jack's friends have gradually reduced in frequency since the time of his accident, and recently Jack has said that he no longer wants any visitors. Jack is also reluctant to go out, leaving the house only for appointments. He previously enjoyed going to watch the rugby at the pub. However, he no longer wishes to do this and appears bored, listless and unhappy. Last month, Jack told his parents that he did not want them to bring Jayden to see him any more, describing himself as an 'embarrassment'. Jack has been losing weight and many of the clothes that he likes to wear (rugby tops, hoodies and jogging bottoms) are much too big for him.

Step 2

The following theories can be usefully applied to Jack's case.

Person-centred approaches

- Key words and phrases – wishes he had never survived the accident; describing himself as an 'embarrassment'.
- Questions – what support might Jack need to rebuild his sense of identity and build a life that he finds more positive?

Strengths-based approaches

- Key words and phrases – worked hard to improve his capabilities; motivated to be discharged.
- Questions – how did Jack demonstrate determination and some key strengths throughout his recovery? How could these strengths be reignited and drawn upon as Jack goes through this difficult time? Are there other people in Jack's life with resources which could be useful in helping him?

Anti-oppressive practice

- Key words and phrases – referring to himself and other people with disabilities using derogatory and oppressive language.
- Questions – how might you be able to challenge Jack's prejudices while demonstrating empathy and understanding for the difficult position he finds himself in? Who in Jack's community might be able to offer him some additional support?

Solution-focused approaches

- Key words and phrases – worked hard to improve his capabilities; motivated to be discharged.
- Questions – how might you work with Jack, his family and his support staff to come up with a way forward? What has worked well for Jack recently and in the past, and what needs to change?

Critically reflective practice

- Key words and phrases – all of the phrases identified so far.
- Questions – how can you reflect on your own position if you have an emotional response to Jack's case? How can you ensure that you are not complicit with discriminatory attitudes? How can you model anti-oppressive values in this situation?

Key words	Person-centred	Strengths-based	Anti-oppressive practice	Solution-focused	Critically reflective practice
Wishes he had never survived the accident	X				X
Describes himself as an embarrassment	X				X
Worked hard to improve his capabilities		X		X	X
Motivated to be discharged		X		X	X
Derogatory about people with disabilities			X		X

Table 2.1 Jack – a summary of key words and phrases, and links with relevant theory

Step 3

Person-centred approaches

From a person-centred perspective, Jack needs to be at the centre of the process, which means focusing on him and what he can do, not on his circumstances or his disability. Jack has suffered major, life-changing physical injuries along with some mild cognitive impairment. His mental health seems to be deteriorating, and he no longer wants to do the things he used to like and that gave him some enjoyment. He doesn't want to go out of the house, meet friends, see his son and he is losing weight. All of this could indicate that he is suffering from depression. Person-centred approaches also argue that Jack's case needs to be viewed holistically.

There are some important people in Jack's life and working in a person-centred way also means focusing on the elements of care and support that matter most not only to Jack but also to his parents, his ex-partner Michaela and their son Jayden. The input of Jack's team of carers will also be important as they have sustained contact with him and are perhaps best placed to know how Jack is on a day-by-day basis.

It seems fair to say that Jack is struggling with his self-concept. Prior to his accident, he probably saw himself as a fit and healthy person who liked a drink. He was lively, funny and a good dad. This all changed drastically and suddenly following his accident. He now might see himself as someone who is completely dependent on other people, an embarrassment, and wishes he hadn't survived the accident. His actualizing tendency seems to be at an all-time low. We know very little about those who are close to him, but they are clearly concerned about his current position.

Listening to Jack using an empathic approach and UPR will be particularly important, in order to build a trusting and non-judgemental relationship with him. It will also be important to gain the trust of his parents, and Jack's carers have an important part to play too in supporting him on a daily basis. This will all take time and commitment to Jack's mental and physical wellbeing. Jack needs to know that his life matters, that he is respected and valued for who he is, and those close to him need to feel this too. The phrase that comes to mind in this case is listen, listen and listen some more, which means asking lots of open questions. This might reveal small ways that Jack can begin to see life more positively, but it is key that these come from him so that he can make progress towards a more positive future.

Strengths-based approaches

Jack is likely to find it difficult to identify his strengths, desires and hopes, and even his strong interests might not be easy for him to discuss in his current frame of mind. Deficit models of disability are relevant to the way Jack now sees himself, as being worthless and an embarrassment. Helping Jack to rebuild his resilience will be key and could be achieved by helping him to find small things that he can be in control of at this point, for example, supporting him in buying a new item of clothing that fits him, which could involve a trip to some shops and trying different things on. However, he has achieved a lot since his accident and initially recovered well through his hard work and determination. Helping him to remember his achievements could be a good starting point, and this can be done by giving him compliments and reminding him of the resilience he has shown.

Using a strengths-based approach, you could ask:

- Survival questions focusing on what helped him initially following his injury. Helping him to remember the support of family and friends that he had in the past could be important in him taking the first steps towards rebuilding these relationships and accessing some resources again.
- Exception questions focusing on any good (or better) times he has at the moment, however small.
- Possibility questions that focus on what he would hope for in the future and how he might be able to take small steps forward to achieve these things.
- Esteem questions about his strengths, abilities and talents. He will probably find this difficult, so he could think about what a good loyal friend might say.

Anti-oppressive practice

Jack has spoken of himself and others with disabilities using derogatory and oppressive language recently. This demonstrates stereotyping and prejudice in his personal attitudes (Thompson's P) in relation to how he sees himself. This will need to be challenged gently and with empathy. This is best achieved by posing some sensitive open questions such as 'What makes you say that?' and by giving examples of the value that people with disabilities can bring to show him an alternative view.

Jack is becoming increasingly isolated, and he needs support with building his community. A good starting point could be charities that offer support groups for people who have experienced life-changing injuries. In addition, there might be other organizations involved in social prescribing in his area that could reach out to Jack and befriend him.

Solution-focused approaches

Setting goals will be important, but any that are set need to be achievable, and they are likely to be small, especially to begin with. Examples of these could be getting out of the house for a short time each day, choosing a small number of food items that he can enjoy as a treat and calling a friend on the phone. He could speak to Jayden on the phone too. Achieving these might help his motivation to be reignited.

Complimenting him on what he has achieved since the accident could be very helpful in building his resilience. He worked hard to be released from hospital and reminding him of how well he did could help him to feel more positive again.

Thinking about exceptions will probably be difficult for Jack at the moment, but he might be able to identify some fleeting moments when he feels better and less pessimistic about his situation.

In time, Jack might be able to respond to the miracle question, but as things stand at the moment, he may well respond by saying that in an ideal world the accident would not have happened, and he would be back to how he was. Posing this question usefully can only be done at the right time.

Critically reflective practice

You might well have an emotional response when working with Jack, so using Gibbs' (1988) reflective cycle could help you to process this. If you find that you are left with some negative feelings in relation to Jack (for example, in the way that he has spoken about people with disabilities), processing these using Boud et al.'s (1985) model could be very useful.

Obviously, you are the only person who can say how you would respond to supporting Jack, and this could be influenced by some particular factors. If you have had personal or professional experience of someone in a similar situation, this could potentially make you assume positive or negative outcomes for Jack. You might be assuming that he can or cannot overcome his current difficulties. Equally, you might be assuming that his parents could or should be doing more to support him and that his friends should be sticking by him, even though this is difficult at the moment. It will be important to ensure that you are not complicit with his discriminatory attitudes by challenging him sensitively. This can be done by asking him sensitive questions like 'What makes you say that?' and by highlighting examples of disabled people who are leading fulfilling lives.

Jack probably feels powerless, and it seems fair to say that everyone involved in his case has more power than he does. But with time, persistence and support, Jack could regain some control over his life.

It could be helpful to read some stories of people who have had similar experiences to Jack in order to understand more of what he faces. You could write notes on your key learning points and discuss these with a colleague, or in supervision.

Case study 2   Cleo

Step 1

Cleo is a 14-year-old young person who has recently been referred to your service after her school raised concerns about the situation at home. Cleo is an only child and lives with her parents in a large house on the outskirts of town. Cleo's parents live an affluent lifestyle, and both work full-time in management roles in the private sector. The family employ an au pair, who takes Cleo to school every morning and cares for her until her parents return home, often late into the evening. At school, Cleo is reported to be a shy child. Academically, she performs very well, and this is supported with private maths tuition, paid for by her parents. She visits her paternal aunt most weekends and enjoys helping to look after her younger cousins. Cleo has always had a close relationship with her aunt and also sees her paternal grandparents regularly.

Cleo's teacher got in touch with your service to express concerns about her emotional wellbeing. Cleo has been described as appearing tearful and having a low sense of self-esteem. She is reported to be easily overwhelmed in new situations and puts a lot of pressure on herself to achieve the best marks in exams. She has also experienced issues within her friendship group, and at times, her behaviour has become disruptive. Some of the older boys have been found to be picking on Cleo, calling her a 'posh kid' and commenting on her body and appearance. The school have punished the boys and offered some pastoral care to Cleo, including a short course on self-esteem and confidence. The quality of Cleo's schoolwork appears to have declined and she seems to be finding it difficult to concentrate. Cleo's teacher contacted her parents, although initially she struggled to get in touch, leaving numerous messages before receiving a response. The teacher described Cleo's mother as 'defensive, cold and dismissive' and commented that she has 'never known any mother who is less interested in her own child'.

You arrange to visit Cleo's family and ask for both parents to be present; however, when you arrive, Cleo's father is not at home. When telling you this news, Cleo's mother refers to her husband as a 'useless waste of space'. You notice that there is a lot of tension between Cleo and her mother. Cleo appears anxious and tearful and will not discuss the referral. Upon hearing about the concerns raised by the school, Cleo's mother becomes angry with her daughter, admonishing her 'poor attitude and behaviour' and stating, 'Everyone can see that Cleo has everything she could ever ask for, not like when I was young, she doesn't know she's born'. When you speak to Cleo alone, she tells you that she feels that nobody cares about her.

Step 2

The following theories can be usefully applied to Cleo's case.

Attachment theory

- Key words and phrases – initially struggled to get in touch; described Cleo's mother as 'defensive, cold and dismissive'; 'never known any mother who is less interested in her own child'; has always had a close relationship with her aunt.
- Questions – what do you notice about the relationship between Cleo and each of her parents? Who do you think are the safe and trusted adults in Cleo's life? What messages about herself, the world and others do you think Cleo has received via her relationship with her primary caregivers?

Feminism

- Key words and phrases – calling her a 'posh kid' and commenting on her body and appearance; described Cleo's mother as 'defensive, cold and dismissive'; 'never known any mother who is less interested in her own child'; 'Everyone can see that Cleo has everything she could ever ask for, not like when I was young, she doesn't know she's born'.
- Questions – how does the teacher's language indicate her views of the role of women in society? Cleo's teacher is very critical of her mother's parenting but does not mention Cleo's father's role in her care. What does this show? What might feminism say about the derogatory comments made to Cleo by older boys?

Psychodynamic approaches

- Key words and phrases – Cleo's mother refers to her husband as a 'useless waste of space'; appearing tearful and having a low sense of self-esteem; easily overwhelmed in new situations and puts a lot of pressure on herself to achieve the best marks in exams; anxious and tearful.
- Questions – what might you want to know about the relationship between Cleo's parents if you were to support this family? How might learning about Cleo's mother's own experience of childhood help you to understand more about her approach to parenting? How might psychodynamic approaches help us to understand Cleo's recent behavioural changes and the behaviour of the older boys?

Cognitive-behavioural approaches

- Key words and phrases – appearing tearful and having a low sense of self-esteem; easily overwhelmed in new situations; nobody cares about her; puts a lot of pressure on herself to achieve the best marks in exams.

○ Questions – how does the ABCDE model apply to Cleo? What is the evidence for Cleo's cycles of negative thinking? How might you help Cleo to set goals and tasks? How might this change her behaviour and feelings?

Critically reflective practice

○ Key words and phrases – all of the phrases identified so far; concerns about her emotional wellbeing; issues within her friendship group and at times her behaviour has become disruptive; quality of Cleo's schoolwork appears to have declined.

Key words	Attachment theory	Feminism	Psychodynamics	Cognitive-behavioural	Critically reflective practice
Initially struggled to get in touch	X				X
Defensive, cold and dismissive	X	X			X
No interest in Cleo	X	X			X
Close relationship with aunt	X				X
Posh kid and comments on body image		X			X
Cleo has everything she could ask for		X			X
Useless waste of space (father)			X		X
Tearful and low sense of self-esteem			X	X	X
Easily overwhelmed			X	X	X
Puts a lot of pressure on herself			X	X	X
Anxious			X		X
Nobody cares about her				X	
Concerns about Cleo's emotional wellbeing					X
Issues with her friendship groups					X
Quality of academic work					X

Table 2.2 Cleo – a summary of key words and phrases, and links with relevant theory

- Questions – which particular reflective cycles might be most useful and why? How might your values affect how you work with Cleo? What assumptions might you be making? Who holds the power in this situation? How might you reflect on the experience of working with Cleo?

Step 3

Attachment theory

Cleo's relationship with her parents can be described as distant and her parents are largely absent from her everyday life. They work long hours during the week and the au pair looks after her during this time. She also seems to see little of them at the weekend. Cleo's relationship with her mother seems difficult, and there is clearly some tension between them. Cleo's mother feels that Cleo has everything she needs, and this is the case materially, but obviously Cleo needs support, care and love as well. There is no information about Cleo's relationship with her father, but clearly her parents are struggling in their own relationship because of the way that her mother speaks about her father as a 'useless waste of space'.

Cleo is likely to have received negative messages from her mother resulting in an avoidant attachment style. This means that she prefers to be at a distance from people, is generally reserved and in this instance, she won't discuss the referral. Her avoidant style also means she enjoys practical things, like looking after her younger cousins, but that she plays down her own needs, preferring not to discuss them.

We don't know anything about Cleo's relationship with the family's au pair or her father, but the safe and trusted adults in Cleo's life seem to be her paternal aunt and her paternal grandparents. She seems to have a good relationship with her young cousins too. It is worth noting that all these people are related to her father. She does not appear to have any close relationships with people on her mother's side of the family.

Feminism

Cleo's teacher uses strong words and is very critical when she describes Cleo's mother as 'defensive, cold and dismissive'. In addition, her comment that she has 'never known any mother who is less interested in her own child' could well have been said with some disdain. The teacher clearly feels that as a mother, she should be more loving and caring towards Cleo, echoing patriarchal messages that assert that this is how mothers are meant to feel and behave. Underneath this, she might also be thinking that Cleo's mother should be at home more often, in a less demanding job where she can give more time and attention to her family, because all of this is more important than money. Cleo's teacher doesn't mention her father in relation to caring for Cleo, which indicates that she feels that the role of primary caregiver is for women only. There is no suggestion that Cleo's father has caring responsibilities too.

The derogatory comments made by the boys at school show that they are objectifying Cleo as a young woman. They are treating her as a thing to be commented on, not as a human being with feelings. There are no details of the comments that have been made on her body and appearance, but these could show their view of Cleo as an object meant for sexual gratification. Equally they could be about the ways in which her appearance fails to meet their ideas of what a young woman should look like. Both of these could be assumptions. However, all of this is probably contributing to her feelings of low self-esteem and is clearly upsetting her. It could also be exacerbating the current dip in her academic performance.

Psychodynamic approaches

The concept of defence mechanisms could be very relevant in understanding various aspects of the relationship between Cleo's parents, and between Cleo and her mother. Cleo's parents' relationship certainly seems somewhat unhealthy on the surface, especially in the way that Cleo's mother talks about her father. There could be any number of reasons for this, and her mother's anger and frustration might be related to this, or it might not. For example, she might be having a really difficult time at work, which comes to the surface when she talks about her husband (displacement), because deep down she feels he could and should do more at home to support her. Equally, she might have had a difficult relationship with her own mother when she was a teenager and might have felt rejected by her in some way. It could be that she can now see this playing out in her relationship with Cleo, which is painful for her (transference). Spending lots of time at work could again be a defence mechanism that stops her from dwelling on this. Of course, these could all be assumptions, and we don't know because we aren't told.

Using free association could be helpful for Cleo's mother and for Cleo herself, giving them the opportunity to speak freely about what might lie beneath their responses. It could help Cleo's father too. We should never underestimate the impact of being listened to, and in many ways, this is what Cleo's case is crying out for.

The older boys at school could be demonstrating the defence mechanism of projection. Calling Cleo a 'posh kid' and making fun of her could be because deep down they would like to have what she has materially, but they might also wish they could be doing as well at school as she is or was. Their behaviour could be pushing Cleo into denial, where she is now not working as hard as she used to, in order to appear less able than she actually is.

Cognitive-behavioural approaches

The ABCDE model could apply to Cleo in this way.

Activating event
Cleo has had some negative experiences. For example, she has been taunted by older boys and her mother has admonished her for the decline in her schoolwork. Both of these things could have happened over a period of time.

Belief system
Cleo is beginning to lack self-belief and her self-confidence is declining. She believes nobody cares about her. In addition she may be starting to have a negative body image.

Consequences
The standard of Cleo's behaviour is declining too; she feels overwhelmed and can't concentrate. Her schoolwork is suffering.

Disputing irrational beliefs
The teacher's suggestion of a short course in self-esteem and confidence could help Cleo dispute some of her irrational beliefs.

Effects
Cleo might begin to see herself differently.

Cleo demonstrates a number of aspects that show she is thinking negatively about herself and her situation. She is often anxious and tearful and is easily overwhelmed by new situations. She lacks confidence in herself and in her abilities, even though she has achieved well in the past. She doesn't want to talk about the referral and the things being suggested that might help her.

Helping Cleo to set some achievable goals could be beneficial and these could help her to begin to think about herself more positively. For example, she could work towards small improvements in her schoolwork, which could restore some of her self-confidence. She could agree to starting the suggested courses to see whether they help her or not. The courses might help her with interpreting her thoughts, feelings and behaviour, thereby breaking her negative cycles of thinking. Some one-to-one mentoring support during and following the course could do this too.

Critically reflective practice

How you respond to Cleo's case will undoubtedly be linked with your own experiences as a teenager and even during your childhood. For example, if you were bullied at school, you might well have an emotional response, so using Gibbs' reflective cycle could help you to process this. Equally, if you have had personal or professional experience of a young person in a similar situation, this could potentially make you assume positive or negative outcomes for Cleo and her family. For example, you might assume that Cleo's parents need to do more to support her, or you might assume that Cleo needs to be more grateful for what she has. Analysing all of this using the Integrated Reflective Cycle (Bassot, 2020) could be helpful, as would writing about this process in a reflective journal.

Cleo probably feels powerless in this situation, but with encouragement and support, she could regain some of the control over her present and future circumstances. It could be helpful to read some literature on the difficulties faced by teenagers in order to understand more of what she faces. You could also research some websites of organizations that support teenagers through adolescence.

Case study 3   The Garside-Rhodes family

Step 1

Tommy Garside (33 years) and Jessica Rhodes (32 years) are the parents of five young children. They all live together in a three-bedroom, privately rented property. The girls, Zoe (10 years old), Carmel (8 years) and Tamsin (3 years), share one bedroom, and 5-year-old twin boys, Leo and Henry, share another bedroom. Tommy has struggled with alcohol misuse on and off since his teens. This has meant that Tommy has struggled to work consistently, and sometimes uses the family budget for alcohol. He is currently experiencing a period of low mood and is drinking daily. A referral is made to the children's social work service by a neighbour who saw the children being cared for by Tommy, who appeared very drunk in the garden, while Jessica was working an evening shift cleaning at the local school.

As there is no telephone number on the referral, you make an unannounced visit to the family home with a colleague during school hours. Although a surprise for the family, they do let you in and want to know what the visit is about. Tamsin is the only child present, and she sits between her parents on the settee, appearing happy and relaxed. You notice that the living room is very sparsely furnished, with just one settee and a TV. There are no signs of any toys or games for the children, and no carpets. It also feels very cold and damp in the property.

Tommy becomes a little defensive when you share the neighbour's concerns. He reports he mainly drinks cans of beer slowly throughout the day, stating 'I can stop drinking any time I want'. He disagrees with the description of himself as having been 'drunk' as reported by the neighbour. Jessica says, 'He just needs some help again. He's a good dad'. Jessica agrees she will not leave the children with Tommy while she works and will ask her sister Jeanette to help. Jessica says she has a large extended family locally but doesn't like them all to know about Tommy's alcohol misuse and only trusts Jeanette.

The next day, you return and speak to each child individually in the kitchen. You can see the property is in poor condition. There is mould on the walls and the cupboard doors are falling off. Zoe says to you, 'Dad does drink every day, but he's ok. He just sleeps a lot. Sometimes he goes out and doesn't come home and mum is a bit worried. He always comes back'. Zoe appears to be a mature child for her age. Carmel is shy and doesn't want to speak to you. Tamsin is very young, but you ask about her favourite toys. Tamsin shows you some cars and a plastic garage which is broken, explaining that her brother Leo stood on it. Leo and Henry are very confident and chatty, talking about school and their friends. They take you upstairs to see the children's bedrooms. All the children have beds and clean bedding, but there are no carpets or curtains. Clothes are stacked on the floor as there is no storage.

Jessica shares that the landlord will not complete any repairs and that they have been on the council waiting list to move to a new property for two years. There is a lot of anti-social behaviour in the area, and she doesn't like the children playing on the street. Jessica feels they are 'stuck in this house' and this is having a negative impact on Tommy's mental health and alcohol use, and Jessica states she is now also 'feeling low' and 'trapped'.

Step 2

The following theories can be usefully applied to this family's case.

Motivational interviewing

- Key words and phrases – struggled with alcohol misuse; struggled to work consistently; a period of low mood and is drinking daily; 'stuck in this house'; negative impact on Tommy's mental health and alcohol use; Jessica is now also 'feeling low' and 'trapped'.
- Questions – how might you engage with Tommy to build a positive relationship? What type of MI techniques might you use to help Tommy focus on positives? How might you help Tommy and Jessica to set goals?

Critical practice

- Key words and phrases – struggled to work consistently; the living room is very sparsely furnished; no signs of any toys or games for the children, and no carpets; feels very cold and damp; mould on the walls and the cupboard doors are falling off; no carpets or curtains; the landlord will not complete any repairs; on the council waiting list to move to a new property for two years; a lot of anti-social behaviour in the area.
- Questions – what might some of the structural or 'root causes' of the family's current situation be? What community resources might be accessed to strengthen the family's support locally?

Systems theory

- Key words and phrases – Jessica's sister Jeanette; Jessica's large extended family; the landlord; the council.
- Questions – how might you encourage the family to engage with their network of family and friends to provide support? How might other existing agencies help to support the family, such as housing and school? Which other professionals or agencies may be able to help?

Critically reflective practice

- Key words and phrases – all of the phrases identified so far; Tommy becomes a little defensive; he disagrees with the description of himself; 'He just needs some help again. He's a good dad'; 'Dad does drink every day, but he's ok. He just sleeps a lot. Sometimes he goes out and doesn't come home and mum is a bit worried. He always comes back'; Zoe appears to be a mature child for her age.
- Questions – which particular reflective cycles might be most useful and why? How might your values affect how you work with this family? What assumptions might you be making? Who holds the power in this situation? How might you reflect on the experience of working with this family?

Key words	Motivational interviewing	Critical practice	Systems theory	Critically reflective practice
Struggled with alcohol misuse	X			X
Struggled to work consistently	X	X		X
A period of low mood and is drinking daily	X			X
Stuck in the house	X			X
Negative impact on Tommy's mental health and alcohol use	X			X
Jessica is now also feeling low and trapped	X			X
The living room is very sparsely furnished		X		X
No signs of any toys or games for the children		X		X
No carpets or curtains		X		X
Feels very cold and damp		X		X
Mould on the walls and the cupboard doors are falling off		X		X
The landlord will not complete any repairs		X	X	X
On the council waiting list to move to a new property for two years		X	X	X
A lot of anti-social behaviour in the area		X		X

Jessica's sister Jeanette			X	X
Jessica's large extended family			X	X
Tommy becomes a little defensive				X
He disagrees with the description of himself				X
'He just needs some help again. He's a good dad', 'Dad does drink every day, but he's ok. He just sleeps a lot.'				X
'Sometimes he goes out and doesn't come home and mum is a bit worried. He always comes back.'				X
Zoe appears to be a mature child for her age				X

Table 2.3 The Garside-Rhodes family – a summary of key words and phrases, and links with relevant theory

Step 3

Motivational interviewing

Tommy probably doesn't recognize that he has a drink problem because he says, 'I can stop drinking any time I want'. This might be the case, or he could be in the Pre-contemplation stage of Prochaska and DiClemente's (1983) model. In order to make progress, Tommy needs to feel accepted by someone with empathy and a non-judgemental and compassionate approach, and working in partnership with him can facilitate this. He needs support to see himself more clearly to identify areas for change. Tommy is the expert on his own life and knows what he can and can't achieve. He knows what works for him and what doesn't, and he needs support to set realistic and achievable goals and to evoke commitment to change. Jessica may well benefit from this kind of approach too, as she appears worn down by her current situation.

A variety of MI techniques could help Tommy, including:

○ Focusing on positive aspects of change that he might have experienced in the past to help him to roll with resistance.
○ Pointing out differences between his current negative experience and the past when his experiences might have been more positive, in order to highlight discrepancies.
○ Discussing times in the past when he drank less in order to support his levels of self-efficacy.

- Using excellent interpersonal skills to ensure he feels listened to and respected, including open questions that allow him to tell his story, reflecting back and summaries.
- Using affirmations to remind him of what he has achieved in the past.

Critical practice

Much of the family's current situation seems to be caused by poverty and exclusion. They clearly have very little income, which is exacerbated by Tommy's drinking habit. Their living conditions are poor, and they don't have some things that could be seen as basic for a comfortable home, such as carpets and toys for the children. The family probably feels powerless in their situation because they have been on the council waiting list for two years, and their landlord will not carry out any repairs. The council and their landlord hold the power to change key practical aspects of their lives for the better.

Hopefully, there are some community resources that can help to improve their situation. There might be other community organizations that support people in poverty, such as a local food bank, charities that can offer other necessary goods such as furniture and bedding and some kind of residents' association. The children's school could also be in touch with organizations who can help and the neighbour who raised concerns and Jessica's sister Jeanette might know of others too.

Systems theory

The family could be supported in order to engage with a variety of networks that might be able to improve their lives. At the macro level, they might be entitled to more benefits than they are currently receiving, and someone from a local citizens' advice bureau could advise them on this.

The meso level includes organizations that they have regular contact with, which includes the children's school and Tamsin's nursery or pre-school, assuming she attends one. Staff here are likely to have contact with organizations in the community that help families with essentials for children, such as clothes, bedding and toys. They might also know where the family could access affordable childcare, which might be paid for as part of their benefits. In addition, there might be organizations that work with people who have issues with alcohol, that in time, Tommy might be prepared to engage with. Ideally, they might have a support group he could join, and they might offer support for partners too. Other community agencies and charities might be able to help with support for people in food and fuel poverty. But the family will probably need support and advocacy to engage with these organizations, which means making initial contacts for them, booking appointments, and even accompanying them to make sure they can access what they need and are entitled to by asking the right questions.

At the meso level, there will be some support from Jessica's sister, and there is the possibility of some from her wider family. However, the latter can only be explored with Jessica, and any contact made must be done with her permission. In time, there might be scope for a meeting with the wider family too, but only when Tommy and Jessica are happy for this to happen. This could give a useful range of perspectives on their situation and could broaden their network of support further.

Critically reflective practice

There is no doubt that this family's situation is extremely challenging and supporting them to find ways of improving their lives will not be easy. As a result, you might make any number of assumptions about the likelihood of being able to support them so that they can all experience a more positive future.

How you respond to the family's situation will be individual to you and using Mezirow's (1978, 1981) seven levels of reflection and Argyris and Schön's (1974) double loop learning cycle could be very valuable in helping you to analyse any assumptions you might be making. Your own personal values are likely to come into play too: those things that you have grown up to think and believe to be important. At a very basic level, whether you had a safe and secure childhood or not, you will be able to see the importance of this for the children. Some of the key words identified might (or might not) chime with your personal experiences. For example, Zoe is the oldest child who is described as mature for her age. Even if you weren't the oldest child, if this phrase was used to describe you, it could prompt memories and feelings through transference. This could particularly be the case if you have experience of alcohol misuse or abuse in your own family. Equally, you might find yourself feeling positive or negative things about certain family members based on previous repressed feelings from other experiences in your personal life through counter-transference. These are worth exploring using the cycles of Gibbs (1988) or Boud et al. (1985).

The family are relatively powerless in their current situation, and the children's safety and overall wellbeing are especially important in this case. Reflecting on your own position in relation to power is important, and this is probably best done in supervision. Preparing for this is also important, so returning to the case notes you have written and analysing them in a reflective journal is likely to be very helpful.

Part 3
From my own practice to theory

Part 3 gives you the opportunity to write your own case studies from your experience in the workplace and to examine them in relation to theory by following three stepping stones.

Step 1 – write your own complex case study from your experience in the workplace

Step 2 – respond to some key questions to identify which theories apply to your case study

Step 3 – use the space provided to write a discussion of how theories apply to your own case study

Case Study 1

Step 1   Your own case study

Use this space to write your own case study from your experience in the workplace.

Step 2   Which theories apply to your case study?

Use the following questions to establish which theories apply best to your case study:
- Which key words and phrases can you identify that give you some indications of which theories apply to your case study?

- Which psychological approaches are most appropriate – those that focus on the past, the future, or both?

- Which sociological approaches are most appropriate?

- How do person-centred approaches apply to this case?

- Which particular aspects of critically reflective practice are important in this case study?

Step 3 Write a discussion of how theories apply to your case study

Use the space provided to write a discussion of how theories apply to your own case study

Case Study 2

Step 1 Your own case study
Use this space to write your own case study from your experience in the workplace.

Step 2 Which theories apply to your case study?
Use the following questions to establish which theories apply best to your case study:
- Which key words and phrases can you identify that give you some indications of which theories apply to your case study?

From my own practice to theory

- Which psychological approaches are most appropriate – those that focus on the past, the future, or both?

- Which sociological approaches are most appropriate?

- How do person-centred approaches apply to this case?

- Which particular aspects of critically reflective practice are important in this case study?

Step 3 Write a discussion of how theories apply to your case study

Use the space provided to write a discussion of how theories apply to your own case study

Case Study 3

Step 1 Your own case study
Use this space to write your own case study from your experience in the workplace.

Step 2 Which theories apply to your case study?
Use the following questions to establish which theories apply best to your case study:
- Which key words and phrases can you identify that give you some indications of which theories apply to your case study?

- Which psychological approaches are most appropriate – those that focus on the past, the future, or both?

- Which sociological approaches are most appropriate?

- How do person-centred approaches apply to this case?

- Which particular aspects of critically reflective practice are important in this case study?

Step 3 Write a discussion of how theories apply to your case study

Use the space provided to write a discussion of how theories apply to your own case study

Case Study 4

Step 1   Your own case study
Use this space to write your own case study from your experience in the workplace.

Step 2   Which theories apply to your case study?
Use the following questions to establish which theories apply best to your case study:
- Which key words and phrases can you identify that give you some indications of which theories apply to your case study?

From my own practice to theory

- Which psychological approaches are most appropriate – those that focus on the past, the future, or both?

- Which sociological approaches are most appropriate?

- How do person-centred approaches apply to this case?

- Which particular aspects of critically reflective practice are important in this case study?

Step 3 Write a discussion of how theories apply to your case study

Use the space provided to write a discussion of how theories apply to your own case study

Case Study 5

Step 1 Your own case study
Use this space to write your own case study from your experience in the workplace.

Step 2 Which theories apply to your case study?
Use the following questions to establish which theories apply best to your case study:
- Which key words and phrases can you identify that give you some indications of which theories apply to your case study?

- Which psychological approaches are most appropriate – those that focus on the past, the future, or both?

- Which sociological approaches are most appropriate?

- How do person-centred approaches apply to this case?

- Which particular aspects of critically reflective practice are important in this case study?

Step 3 Write a discussion of how theories apply to your case study

Use the space provided to write a discussion of how theories apply to your own case study

Case Study 6

Step 1 Your own case study

Use this space to write your own case study from your experience in the workplace.

Step 2 Which theories apply to your case study?

Use the following questions to establish which theories apply best to your case study:
- Which key words and phrases can you identify that give you some indications of which theories apply to your case study?

From my own practice to theory

- Which psychological approaches are most appropriate – those that focus on the past, the future, or both?

- Which sociological approaches are most appropriate?

- How do person-centred approaches apply to this case?

- Which particular aspects of critically reflective practice are important in this case study?

Step 3 Write a discussion of how theories apply to your case study

Use the space provided to write a discussion of how theories apply to your own case study

Further reading

Al-Ma'seb, H. Alkhurinej, A. and Alduwaihi, M. (2015) 'The gap between theory and practice in social work', *International Social Work*, 58 (6): 819–30.

Beckett, C. and Horner, N. (2016) *Essential Theory for Social Work Practice*, 2nd edn, London: Sage.

Beckett, C. and Taylor, H. (2019) *Human Growth and Development*, 4th edn, London: Sage.

Deacon, L. and Macdonald, S. J. (2017) *Social Work Theory and Practice*, London: Learning Matters/Sage.

Heslop, P. and Meredith, C. (2021) *Social Work Theory in Practice*, London: Sage.

Kaprowska, J. (2020) *Communication and Interpersonal Skills in Social Work*, 5th edn, London: Learning Matters/Sage.

Maclean, S. and Harrison, R. (2015) *Theory and Practice: A Straightforward Guide for Social Work Students*, 3rd edn, Lichfield: Kirwin McLean Associates.

Stepney, P. and Thompson, N. (2021) 'Isn't it time to start "theorising practice" rather than trying to "apply theory to practice"?', *Practice*, 33 (2): 149–63.

Thompson, N. and Stepney, P. (2017) *Social Work Theory and Methods: The Essentials*, Abingdon: Routledge.

References

Ainsworth, M., Blehar, M., Waters, E. and Wall, S. (1978) *Patterns of Attachment: Psychological Study of the Strange Situation*, Hillsdale: Erlbaum.

Argyris, C. and Schön, D. (1974) *Theory in Practice: Increasing Professional Effectiveness*, San Francisco: Jossey-Bass.

Bandura, A. (1977) *Social Learning Theory*, Englewood Cliffs: Prentice Hall.

Bandura, A. (1986) *Social Foundations of Thought and Action: A Social Cognitive Theory*, Englewood Cliffs: Prentice Hall.

Bassot, B. (2020) *The Reflective Journal*, 3rd edn, London: Red Globe Press.

Beck, A. T. (1967) *Depression: Causes and Treatment*, Philadelphia: University of Pennsylvania Press.

Beckett, C. and Horner, N. (2016) *Essential Theory for Social Work Practice*, 2nd edn, London: Sage.

Beesley, P., Watts, M. and Harrison, M. (2018) *Developing your Communication Skills in Social Work*, London: Sage.

Bell, D. L. and Roomaney, R. (2020) 'Exploring the barriers that prevent practitioners from implementing motivational interviewing in their work with clients', *Social Work*, 56 (4): 416–29.

Berzoff, J. (2011) 'Psychodynamic theory and gender', in J. Berzoff, L. Melano Flanagan and P. Hertz (eds), *Inside Out and Outside: Psychodynamic Clinical Theory and Psychopathology in Contemporary Multicultural Contexts*, 241–57, Lanham: Rowman & Littlefield.

Blakemore, S-J. and Frith, U. (2005) *The Learning Brain: Lessons for Education*, Oxford: Blackwell.

Boud, D., Keogh, R. and Walker, D. (1985) *Reflection: Turning Experience into Learning*, London: RoutledgeFalmer.

Bowlby, J. (1969) *Attachment and Loss, Volume 1: Attachment*, London: Hogarth Press.

Brookfield, D. S. (1995) *Becoming a Critically Reflective Teacher*, San Francisco: Jossey-Bass.

Cocker, C. and Hafford-Letchfield, T. (2014) 'Introduction: Rethinking anti-discriminatory and anti-oppressive practice in social work; time for new paradigms', in C. Cocker and T. Hafford-Letchfield (eds), *Rethinking Anti-discriminatory and Anti-oppressive Theories for Social Work*, 1–19, Basingstoke: Palgrave Macmillan.

Corey, G., Schneider Corey, M. and Callanan, P. (2007) *Issues and Ethics in the Helping Professions*, 7th edn, Belmont: Thomson Brooks/Cole.

Criado Perez, C. (2020) *Invisible Women: Exposing Data Bias in a World Designed for Men*, London: Vintage.

Davis, A. Y. (2019) *Women, Race and Class*, London: Penguin Books.

de Shazer, S. (1985) *Keys to Solution in Brief Therapy*, New York: Norton.

Dewey, J. (1933) *How We Think: A Restatement of the Relation of Reflective Thinking to the Educative Process*, Boston: D. C. Heath & Co.

Dominelli, L. (2002) *Anti-oppressive Social Work Theory and Practice*, Basingstoke: Palgrave Macmillan.

Ellis, A. (1962) *Reason and Emotion in Psychotherapy*, New York: Stuart.

Fook, J. (2007) 'Reflective practice and critical reflection', in J. Lishman (ed.), *Handbook for Practice Learning in Social Work and Social Care: Knowledge and Theory*, 2nd edn, 363–75, London: Jessica Kingsley.

Fook, J. (2022) *Social Work: A Critical Approach to Practice*, 4th edn, London: Sage.

Fook, J. and Gardner, F. (2007) *Practising Critical Reflection: A Resource Handbook*, Maidenhead: Open University Press.

Foster, J. (2018) 'Feminist movement histories', in S. Butler-Mokoro and L. Grant (eds), *Feminist Perspectives on Social Work Practice: The Intersecting Lives of Women in the 21st Century*, 33–58, New York: Oxford University Press.

Foucault, M. (1977) *Discipline and Punish: The Birth of the Prison*, Harmondsworth: Penguin.

Gabbard, G. O. (2014) *Psychodynamic Psychiatry in Clinical Practice*, 5th edn, Washington, DC: American Psychiatric Publishing.

Gaudiano, B. A. (2008) 'Cognitive-behavioural therapies: Achievements and challenges', *Evidence- Based Mental Health*, 11 (1): 5–7.

Gibbs, G. (1988) *Learning by Doing: A Guide to Teaching and Learning Methods*, Oxford: Further Education Unit, Oxford Polytechnic.

Gibson, R. (1986) *Critical Theory and Education*, London: Hodder & Stoughton.

Goldstein, H. (1975) 'Some critical observations on the relevance of social systems theory for social work practice', *Canadian Journal of Social Work Education/Revue Canadienne d'éducation En Service Social*, 1 (3): 13–23.

Goodman, J. (1992) 'Towards a discourse of imagery: Critical curriculum theorizing', *The Educational Forum*, 56 (3): 269–89.

Gray, M. (2011) 'Back to basics: A critique of the strengths perspective in social work', *Families in Society*, 92 (1): 5–11.

Hanna, D. (1997) 'The organization as an open system', in A. Harris, N. Bennett and M. Preedy (eds), *Organizational Effectiveness and Improvement in Education*, Buckingham: Open University Press.

Hazan, C. and Shaver, P. R. (1994) 'Deeper into attachment theory', *Psychological Inquiry*, 5 (1): 68–79.

Healy, K. (2014) *Social Work Theories in Context*, 2nd edn, Basingstoke: Palgrave Macmillan.

Higgins, G. (1994) *Resilient Adults: Overcoming a Cruel Past*, San Francisco: Jossey-Bass.

Howe, D. (2009) *A Brief Introduction to Social Work Theory*, London: Palgrave.

Illeris, K. (2014) *Transformative Learning and Identity*, Abingdon: Routledge.

Ixer, G. (1999) 'There's no such thing as reflection', *British Journal of Social Work*, 29 (4): 513–27.

Jewson, N. and Mason, D. (1986) 'The theory and practice of equal opportunities policies: Liberal and radical approaches', *The Sociological Review*, 34 (2): 307–34.

Joseph, S. (2003) 'Why the client knows best', *The Psychologist*, 16 (6): 304–7.

Kisthardt, W. E. (2013) 'Integrating the core competencies in strengths-based, person-centred practice: Clarifying purposes and reflecting principles', in D. Saleebey (ed.), *The Strengths Perspective in Social Work Practice*, 6th edn, 23–78, Boston: Pearson.

Kolb, D. (1984) *Experiential Learning: Experience as the Source of Learning and Development*, Upper Saddle River: Prentice Hall.

Kondrat, D. C. and Miller, K. (2020) 'Solution-focused practice', in B. Teater (ed.), *An Introduction to Applying Social Work Theories and Models*, 3rd edn, 162–77, London: Open University Press.

Lewin, K. (1951) 'Problems of research in social psychology', in D. Cartwright (ed.), *Field Theory in Social Science: Selected Theoretical Papers*, 155–69, New York: Harper & Row.

Loughran, H. (2019) *Counselling Skills for Social Workers*, Abingdon: Routledge.

Luty, J. and Iwanowicz, M. (2018) 'Motivational interviewing: Living up to its promise?', *BJPsych Advances*, 24 (1): 46–53.

Maier, S. F. and Seligman, M. E. P. (2016) 'Learned helplessness at fifty: Insights from neuroscience', *Psychological Review*, 123 (4): 349–67.

Maslow, A. H. (1943) 'A theory of human motivation', *Psychological Review*, 50 (4): 370–96.

Masson, J. (1988) *Against Therapy: Emotional Tyranny and the Myth of Psychological Healing*, London: Collins.

Mattei, L. (2011) 'Coloring development: Race and culture in psychodynamic theories', in J. Berzoff, L. Melano Flanagan and P. Hertz (eds), *Inside Out and Outside: Psychodynamic Clinical Theory and Psychopathology in Contemporary Multicultural Contexts*, 258–83, Lanham: Rowman & Littlefield.

McLaughlin, J. (2003) *Feminist Social and Political Theory: Contemporary Debates and Dialogues*, London: Red Globe Press.

McLaughlin, K. (2016) *Empowerment: A Critique*, Abingdon: Routledge.

Mental Health Act (1983) Available at https://www.legislation.gov.uk/ukpga/1983/20/contents (accessed 5 October 2023).

Mesters, I. (2009) 'Editorial: Motivational interviewing: Hype or hope?', *Chronic Illness*, 5 (1): 3–6.

Meyer, C. (1976) *Social Work Practice*, New York: Free Press.

Mezirow, J. (1978) *Education for Perspective Transformation: Women's Reentry Programs in Community Colleges*, New York: Centre for Adult Education, Columbia University.

Mezirow, J. (1981) 'A critical theory of adult learning and education', *Adult Education*, 32 (1): 13–24.

Miller, W. R. and Rollnick, S. (2013) *Motivational Interviewing: Helping People Change*, New York: Guilford Press.

Milliken, E. (2017) 'Feminist theory in social work practice', in F. J. Turner (ed.), *Social Work Treatment: Interlocking Theoretical Approaches*, 6th edn, 191–208, New York: Oxford University Press.

Musson, P. (2017) *Making Sense of Theory and its Application in Social Work Practice*, St Albans: Critical Publishing.

Neenan, M. and Dryden, W. (2021) *Cognitive Behaviour Therapy: 100 Key points*, 3rd edn, Abingdon: Routledge.

Pavlov, I. P. (1928) *Lectures on Conditioned Reflexes*, trans. W. H. Gantt, London: Allen & Unwin.

Payne, M. (2020) *How to Use Social Work Theory in Practice: An Essential Guide*, Bristol: Policy Press.

Payne, M. (2021) *Modern Social Work Theory*, 5th edn, London: Red Globe Press.

Pérez Alonso, M. A. (2015) 'Metacognition and sensorimotor components underlying the process of handwriting and keyboarding and their impact on learning: An analysis from the perspective of embodied psychology', *Procedia – Social and Behavioral Sciences*, 176: 263–69.

Prochaska, J. O. and DiClemente, C. C. (1983) 'Stages and processes of self-change of smoking: Toward an integrative model of change', *Journal of Consulting and Clinical Psychology*, 51 (3): 390–5.

Redfern, C. and Aune, K. (2013) *Reclaiming the F Word: Feminism Today*, London: Zed Books.

Robbins, P., Chatterjee, P. and Canda, E. R. (2006) *Contemporary Human Behavior Theory: A Critical Perspective for Social Work*, 2nd edn, Boston: Pearson.

Rogers, C. (1951) *Client-centred Therapy: Its Current Practice, Implications and Theory*, Boston: Houghton Mifflin

Rogers, C. R. (1959) 'A theory of therapy, personality, and interpersonal relationships, as developed in the client-centered framework', in S. Koch (ed.), *Psychology: A Study of a Science: Vol. 3*, 184–256, New York: McGraw Hill.

Rogers, C. R. (1980) *A Way of Being*, Boston: Houghton Mifflin.

Saleebey, D. (1996) 'The strengths perspective in social work practice: Extensions and cautions', *Social Work*, 41 (3): 296–305.

Saleebey, D. (2002) 'Introduction: Power in the people', in D. Saleebey (ed.), *The Strengths Perspective in Social Work Practice*, 3rd edn, 1–22, Boston: Allyn & Bacon.

Saltiel, D. (2010) 'Judgement, narrative and discourse: A critique of reflective practice', in H. Bradbury, N. Frost, S. Kilminster and M. Zukas (eds), *Beyond Reflective Practice: New Approaches to Professional Lifelong Learning*, 130–42, Abingdon: Routledge.

Schön, D. A. (1983) *The Reflective Practitioner*, Aldershot: Ashgate.

Seligman, M. E. P. (1991) *Learned Optimism: How to Change Your Mind and Your Life*, New York: Knopf.

Seligman, M. E. P. and Csikszentmihályi, M. (2000) 'Positive psychology: An introduction', *American Psychologist*, 55 (1): 5–14.

Seligman, M. E. and Maier, S. F. (1967) 'Failure to escape traumatic shock', *Journal of Experimental Psychology*, 74 (1): 1–9.

Sudbery, J. and Whittaker, A. (2019) *Human Growth and Development: An Introduction for Social Workers*, 2nd edn, London: Routledge.

Taylor, E. W. (2009) 'Fostering transformative learning', in J. Mezirow, E. W. Taylor and associates (eds), *Transformative Learning in Practice: Insights from Community, Workplace and Higher Education*, 3–17, San Francisco: Jossey-Bass.

Teater, B. (2020) *An Introduction to Applying Social Work Theories and Models*, 3rd edn, London: Open University Press.

Thomas, G. (2017) *How to do your Research Project: A Guide for Students in Education and Applied Social Sciences*, 3rd edn, London: Sage.

Thompson, N. (2021) *Anti-Discriminatory Practice*, 7th edn, London: Red Globe Press.

Tyson, L. (2014) *Critical Theory: A User-friendly Guide*, 3rd edn, Abingdon: Routledge.

Usher, R and Bryant, I. (1989) *Adult Education as Theory, Practice and Research*, London: Routledge.

Vicedo, M. (2011) 'The social nature of the mother's tie to her child: John Bowlby's theory of attachment in post-war America', *The British Journal for the History of Science*, 44 (3): 401–26.

von Bertalanffy, L. (1968) *General System Theory: Foundations, Development, Applications*, New York: George Braziller.

Walker, C. R., Froerer, A. S. and Gourlay-Fernandez, N. (2022) 'The value of using emotions in solution focused brief therapy', *Journal of Marital and Family Therapy*, 48 (3): 812–26.

Watson, J. B. and Raynor, R. (1920) 'Conditioned emotional reactions', *Journal of Experimental Psychology*, 3 (1): 1–14.

Wendt, S. (2016) 'Conversations about theory: Feminism and social work', in S. Wendt and N. Moulding (eds), *Contemporary Feminisms in Social Work Practice*, 11–23, Abingdon: Routledge.

Wendt, S. (2019) 'Feminist ideas in social work', in M. Payne and E. Reith-Hall (eds), *Routledge Handbook of Social Work Theory*, 361–70, Abingdon: Routledge.

Westergaard, J. (2017) *An Introduction to Helping Skills: Counselling, Coaching and Mentoring*, London: Sage.

Williams, M. and Penman, D. (2011) *Mindfulness: A Practical Guide to Finding Peace in a Frantic World*, London: Piatkus.

Winnicott, D. W. (1960) 'The theory of the parent-infant relationship', *The International Journal of Psychoanalysis*, 41: 585–95.

Yip, K. (2006) 'Self-reflection in reflective practice: A note of caution', *British Journal of Social Work*, 36 (5): 777–88.

Zuffery, C. (2016) 'Homelessness and intersectional feminist practice', in S. Wendt and N. Moulding (eds), *Contemporary Feminisms in Social Work Practice*, 238–48, Abingdon: Routledge.

ABC model   34
ABCDE model   35
Ainsworth et al   23
Anti-discriminatory
    practice   119, 120, 122
Anti-oppressive
    practice   119-30, 159, 161
Argyris and Schön   144, 176
Attachment stages   23-4
Attachment styles
    Ambivalent   25, 29, 33
    Avoidant   23, 28, 33, 165
    Disorganized   25, 29, 33
    Secure   23, 24, 25, 26, 28, 33

Bandura   34, 35, 60
Beck   36
Beckett and Horner   2
Beesley et al   58
Bell and Roomaney   61
Bentham   96
Berzoff   14
Blakemore and Frith   23
Boud et al   143, 151, 162, 176
Bowlby   23, 24, 25
Brookfield   145

Cocker and Hafford-
    Letchfield   122
Compliments   47, 48, 54-5, 57, 75, 80, 161
Congruence   132, 136, 140
Core conditions   132, 133, 136, 140, 142
Corey et al   134
Counter-transference   13, 17, 22, 176
Criado Perez   107

Davis   110
de Shazer   46
Defence mechanisms   12, 16, 17, 20, 21, 168
Dewey   143
Discourses   96-8, 100, 102-3, 105-6, 119, 120, 121, 128
Dominelli   122

Ego   11-12, 16, 19, 21
Ellis   35, 39
Empathy   48, 132, 134, 136, 140, 142, 159, 162, 174
Expressing   60, 67
Empowerment   74, 121, 122

Fook   96, 143
Fook and Gardner   143
Foster   108
Foucault   95, 96
Free association   13, 20, 168
Freud   5, 11, 13, 14

Gabbard   14
Gaudiano   37
Gibbs   143, 151, 162, 169, 176
Gibson   98
Goals   43, 44, 45, 46, 47, 48, 58, 60, 166, 172, 174
    achievable   46, 48, 50, 54, 56, 66, 162, 169
    setting   37, 40
Goldstein   86
Goodman   97
Gray   74

Hanna   86
Hazan and Shaver   26
Healy   84, 85
Higgins   73
Howe   2, 72, 84, 95, 119, 121, 122

Id   11-12, 16, 19, 21
Illeris   143
Intersectionality   109, 115, 126
Ixer   146

Jewson and Mason   109
Joseph   132

Kisthardt   73
Kolb   143
Kondrat and Miller   48

Lewin   5-6
Loughran   58
Luty and Iwanowicz   61

Maier and Seligman   72
Maslow   131
Masson   133
Mattei   14
McLaughlin, J   108
McLaughlin, K   122
Mesters   61
Meyer   85
Mezirow   144, 176
Miller and Rollnick   58
Milliken   108
Miracle question   47, 48, 52, 55, 57, 162
Multicuturalism   119-20
Musson   2

Neenan and Dryden   37

OARS   61
Oppression   96, 98, 107, 108, 109, 110, 119, 120, 122

Panopticon   96-7
Pavlov   34, 72
Payne   2, 86, 108
Pérez Alonso   4
Prochaska and
    DiClemente   58, 63, 66, 69, 174

Questions
    coping   47, 48
    esteem   75, 81, 83, 161
    exception   74, 78, 81, 83, 161
    open   61, 67, 161, 162, 175
    possibility   75, 78, 81, 83, 161
    survival   74, 78, 81, 83, 161

Redfern and Aune   110
Reflexivity   134, 143, 145
Robbins et al   14
Rogers   58, 131-4, 135, 141

Saleebey 74
Saltiel 146
Scaling 46, 54, 56
Schön 145, 176
Self-
  actualize 131
  awareness 145
  concept 131, 133, 136, 139, 141, 160
  efficacy 60, 61, 64, 67, 71
Seligman 73
Seligman and Csikszentmihályi 72
Seligman and Maier 72
Social justice 74, 119, 146

Sudbery and Whitaker 25
Superego 11, 12, 14, 16, 19, 21

Teater 2, 61, 134
Thomas 5, 6
Thompson 95, 120-2, 125, 127, 130, 162
Transference 13, 17, 20, 21, 168, 176
Tyson 97

Unconditional positive regard (UPR) 132, 133-4, 136, 140, 142, 161
Usher and Bryant 146

Vicedo 25
von Bertalanffry 85

Walker et al 48
Watson and Raynor 34
Wendt 26, 108
Westergaard 36
Williams and Penman 145
Winnicott 24
Wollstonecraft 108

Yip 146

Zuffery 110